outstanding in the field

outstanding in the field

A FARM TO TABLE COOKBOOK

To Amy —

Enjoy the fzn

Go - Hawz !!

Jim denevan

WITH MARAH STETS

clarkson potter/publishers

new york

Library of Congress Cataloging-in-Publication Data
Denevan, Jim.
    Outstanding in the field : a farm to table cookbook
/ Jim Denevan with Marah Stets. — 1st ed.
        p.   cm.
    Includes index.
1. Cookery, American—California style. I. Stets,
Marah. II. Title.
TX715.2.C34D36 2008
641.59794—dc22   2007033941

ISBN 978-0-307-38199-6

Printed in China

Principal food photography by Alexandra Grablewski
Principal location photography by Andrea Wyner
Photographs by Tom Brodnax, Chesley Chen,
Alexandra Grablewski, Colleen Sweeney, Andrea
Wyner, and Outstanding in the Field are copyright
© 2008 in the individual photographer's name.

Design by Maggie Hinders

10 9 8 7 6 5 4 3 2 1

First Edition

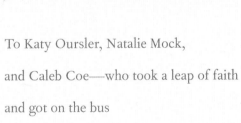

To Katy Oursler, Natalie Mock,

and Caleb Coe—who took a leap of faith

and got on the bus

for our first tour of North America

contents

introduction

EVERY JUNE, a few intrepid companions and I pile into an intermittently reliable 1953 Flxible bus we call Outstanding and spend the next four months driving across North America. At several points along the way we stop for a few nights and get to know the locals in a way that most tourists do not: We set an 80-foot-long table where no table has ever been set and serve dinner under the sky to as many as 100 strangers. These dinners are usually held in the fields of small farms, ranches, dairies, or vineyards, but we've also dined in the belly

of a sea cave, on a disappearing isthmus, and in an urban community garden. Our mission is to help people reconnect to their local land and to the farmers and food artisans who tend it. To that end, the ingredients for these dinners come directly from the fields in which our table sits, and the farmers and food artisans who cultivate those ingredients share equal billing with the chefs and sit shoulder to shoulder with the guests at our long table. It's not every day one gets to sit next to the person who planted the beans, raised the lamb, and shaped the cheese on your plate.

The idea for this roving restaurant came to me in the kitchen of a stationary one. I was chef at the cozy Gabriella Café in Santa Cruz, California, for a number of years. Probably my most beloved time of year was foraging season, which begins in November in Northern California. Foragers spend their days wandering the forests and glades just outside of Santa Cruz and their evenings making the rounds of local restaurants to sell the wild delicacies they've gathered. One of my favorite foragers was, and is, David Chambers. It was David's quirky habit to show up on Saturday night at just about the time when things were getting really busy and plant himself squarely in the middle of the kitchen, holding baskets teeming with treasures such as miner's lettuce, porcini, chanterelles, and nettles. Invigorated by his day of foraging, he regaled anyone who would listen with the stories of his day's harvest—where he'd been, what he'd seen, and why this or that was particularly abundant this year. If, by chance, I wanted to buy a few things for the restaurant's menu, well, that was okay with David, too.

In a typical American restaurant, most ingredients are without provenance or story. The chef simply orders what he or she needs and it shows up. It's inevitable that the cooks respond to that; they don't have a strong connection to the food. For people at home, it's no different. The food at the grocery store may look abundant and even beautiful, but its origins are a mystery to us and we are utterly disconnected from them. We buy fruit, vegetables, meats, fish, and grains; then we bring this bounty home, cook it, and eat it, in many cases without any idea where it grew or was born, how it was cared for, what it was fed, or by what means it was harvested or slaughtered. Above all, we are utterly ignorant of the people responsible for every step on our food's path—and they are numerous: produce, poultry, and dairy farmers, ranchers, fishers, vintners, and foragers. Without these people, there would be no bounty for our tables. It took a few years of those foraging-season visits by David Chambers for it to hit me: We were missing the point. Our culture deifies chefs, but it really isn't the chef whose story should matter so much. It is the farmer, the forager, the artisan producer. I decided that all these people who touch our ingredients before we see them needed a stage of their own.

We started Farmer Dinners at Gabriella Café almost immediately thereafter. We invited local farmers into the restaurant, cooked what they grew, and let them speak directly to the diners. We undertook a new education for our in-house staff as well: We took trips to farms and farmers' markets and went on foraging adventures with guides like David. The Farmer Dinners were a huge success—Gabriella Café still does them, in fact—and the staff and I had never felt more connected to and inspired by the tools of our trade. No longer were the beef and sole and tomatoes just food on our plates; now there were people and places attached to all of them. But it wasn't long before I realized we were only bringing the people half of the story to the patrons at Gabriella Café; the places were still a mystery. It dawned on me that while Farmer Dinners were good, *Farm* Dinners would be better.

Our first farm dinner was held in September 1999 at Andrew Griffin and Julia Wiley's Mariquita Farm in Corallitos, California. Very little about our dinners has changed since then. That night we started one of many traditions: After all of our eighty guests arrived, they walked the fields with Andy and Julia before dinner. It was incredibly moving and inspiring to witness the farmers sharing their fields and their stories with so many rapt visitors. Another enduring tradition was started that day: Only after the farm tour was over did the guests see the long stretch of table, covered in white tablecloths and, on this night, framed by a wall of perfectly ripe tomatoes on one side, a stretch of irises on the other, a floor of earth below, and the wide-open sky far above.

I had persuaded Tom King, a colorful friend of mine who was chef-proprietor at a Santa Cruz restaurant called Papa's Church, to come out on the farm with me to help prepare dinner. For our main dish, we stuffed a 150-pound pig from a local hog farm with plums, sausage, and cabbage; wrapped it tightly in damp cloth; and placed it on hot river rocks buried 3 feet underground for 15 hours. When it was time to eat, we distributed shovels to a few of our guests and enlisted their help digging up the pig. Our dinner also included Potato, Sweet Chile, and Wild Fennel Salad (page 56), made with freshly dug potatoes and chiles from the farm and the wild fennel that is so abundant in Santa Cruz County.

By the end of the dinner, planners and participants alike felt euphoric, our senses heightened by the fresh air and our appetites sated by the delicious food. Thanks to the abundant local wine poured during the meal, we were also a little drunk, which is probably why it took us a bit of time to realize that night had come while we were eating and pitch blackness had fallen all around us. Getting everyone back through the fields to their cars was going to be a challenge, if not nearly impossible. Thankfully—and this was hardly the last time I felt thankful for my wonderfully improvisational, truly outstanding staff—one of my assistants had the wherewithal to locate a stash of tea lights. They were promptly put into service lining a path back to the cars. The sweet peas and tomatoes glowed right along with the rest of us. As we cleaned up by the light of those tea lights, I knew I had found my answer: We had to get as many people as possible out there standing in the fields. With the revelation came the name, and Outstanding in the Field was born.

Since that first dinner, we've hosted dozens more in California and far beyond. We enjoy a sort of perpetual harvest by following the good weather across North America. This means we generally stage our dinners in the late spring through fall. In June and July we begin with several in California, the land of endless summer, or at least a long, rainless summer. In August we head north to Alaska and Canada, turn to the Midwest and Northeast in early September, and then move across the South in early October. We head back to Southern California for some late October dinners, and we end every season with a homecoming foraging dinner in a beautiful and warm refurbished barn after the first rains of November.

Any Outstanding dinners not cooked by me are prepared by local guest chefs. It may seem contradictory to say on the one hand that I started Outstanding in the Field as an antidote to the culture of chef worshipping while on the other hand I speak often and proudly of the fantastic chefs who prepare our dinners. The difference lies in the emphasis: Our dinners are about everyone involved—guest, farmer, even chef—learning something new, not about how much everyone involved already knows. We choose our guest chefs, many of whom are well known locally and even nationally, based on two factors. First, they are all deeply knowledgeable about ingredients and how to cook them, so they are always great sources of inspiration to our guests and especially to the farmers, who are often delighted to see the fruits of their labor transformed into delectable dishes. Second, and perhaps more important, the chefs themselves thrill to the prospect of learning something new in the field or wilderness. Seeing the harvest simultaneously through the eyes of the farmers who sow the bounty and the chefs who reap it is probably the most enlightening aspect of an Outstanding in the Field dinner.

As is true of most high-caliber chefs, all of our guest chefs have relationships with excellent local farmers, foragers, and artisanal producers, but for the most part—restaurant work being an eighteen-hour-a-day pursuit—their ingredients are directly delivered to the kitchen. With notable exceptions, chefs are not regularly able to visit the sources of their ingredients. For everyone involved in an Outstanding in the Field dinner, the magic comes when the walls of the kitchen are removed and a great chef is placed in the field with the farmer or on the edge of the wilderness with little more than a fishing pole. Suddenly the walk-in refrigerator is replaced by rows of fruits, herbs, and vegetables ready for picking, animals roaming freely, or water plentiful with fish, and the land itself becomes the chef's pantry. David Hawksworth of West Restaurant in Vancouver, British Columbia, may best represent what an Outstanding chef is, having caught the salmon himself for one of the three wonderful dinners we've done together.

Plenty of our guest chefs already know that a direct line to the farms gives them the freshest ingredients and the best sources of inspiration. Dan Barber hosted us at Stone Barns, his farm in Pocantico Hills, New York, before the upstate version of his celebrated New York City restaurant, Blue Hill, had opened on the land. At Blue Hill at Stone Barns, farm and restaurant share the same acreage, and the ingredients go directly from field to kitchen to table. Better still, the kitchen and table waste go right back out to the farm and barn to nourish the soil and animals. This endeavor is the very definition of *sustainable food*. On the opposite coast, David Kinch, a two-time guest chef, has

teamed with farmer Cynthia Sandberg of Love Apple Farm to grow biodynamic produce exclusively for his acclaimed restaurant, Manresa, in Los Gatos, California. These chefs and others, including Gabrielle Hamilton and Michael Anthony in New York, Paul Kahan in Chicago, and Mary Dumont in Portsmouth, New Hampshire, care deeply about the provenance of the ingredients used in their restaurants. While a sort of roaming restaurant in the fields is our mission, their mission is to move the bounty inside with as little interference as possible. I'm pleased to note that theirs is a growing movement.

By its nature, Outstanding in the Field emphasizes seasonality and local availability. We travel with the seasons, and we cook what's in the fields. Several days before a farm dinner, we walk the fields with the farmer and guest chef, if there is one, notebooks in hand, so we can touch and smell and bite into what is growing. We plan the menu based on what's ripe in the field—quite easy to do because the ingredients have only a few yards to travel from field to kitchen. But seasonality itself is not fixed, for while seasons are common to everyone, not everyone in North America, or indeed the world, has a common season. Everybody has a different time that is "fall" or "summer" or "spring," foodwise. Furthermore, many fruits and vegetables—raspberries, for example, and many root vegetables—actually have two seasons. Supermarkets confuse the issue by having produce available from everywhere all the time. You can learn what *local seasonality* means by visiting a farmers' market or well-run farm.

Check out Local Harvest (www.localharvest.org) to find these sources close to you, and then get out there and look around.

As far back as I can remember, I have been fascinated by nature's changing seasons and the weather those changes bring. When I was a kid, I dreamed of being a meteorologist. I guess I didn't land so far off the mark. Even if I don't technically study the weather, I certainly do live by the seasons and definitely prefer to set the rhythm of my life to the natural world. I think the fact that I am far happier outside than in is part of what drove me to create a restaurant without walls. I know it led me to my other passion, which began with a few simple lines in the sand. One morning in the summer of 1996, I set my finger down on a beach and drew a 10-foot-long fish. Before long, I'd made half a dozen giant companions for my fish—birds, people, and dinosaurs—quite a merry band of creatures. It was a chaotic time for me. My mother had been struck by Alzheimer's disease, and I was overwhelmed and exhausted by work and life. The hours of that morning melted away as I dragged my finger through the sand, and when the last line was drawn, I walked to the top of a nearby cliff. From high above the beach, I looked down on my enormous canvas. The afternoon sun streamed across the drawings and made them shimmer in the waning light. I stood for a long time and watched passing people—tiny from that distance—weave in and out of my drawings as the incoming tide crept closer with each wave, licking at and erasing the lines. My merry band would be gone by morning. I was flooded by a sensation I'd been missing: peacefulness.

I can't say that continuing to draw was a conscious decision. Since that summer morning, my art is as much a part of me as my body and mind are. I have refined my technique (my finger was pretty sore by the end of that first morning). Nowadays my paintbrushes are an old rake and whatever long stick has washed up on shore. My canvases have been as varied as are the shorelines of North America. My subjects have moved beyond fish and dinosaurs and tend to be quite a bit larger: from a 1,500-foot triangle on the flat sands of Vancouver's Spanish Banks, in sight of that city's breathtaking skyline, to a 600-foot spiral on Rye Beach, near Portsmouth, New Hampshire. I am often asked if I am bothered that after spending up to a full day on a sometimes miles-wide drawing, the tide always comes to wash it away. To me, it is no different than setting a table in a field and inviting strangers to come and eat food harvested only hours before. The art, like the farm tour dinners, is fleeting, but both leave an enduring impression.

Interestingly, whenever I am approached to discuss either my art or the dinners, the questions and the conclusions drawn by the questioner inevitably return to the alleged novelty of both. But although Outstanding in the Field appears unusual, in fact, celebrating the harvest is something we humans did with absolute regularity until fairly recently. What seems exciting now—sharing the bounty of freshly picked ripe food with a community of people—was commonplace before the dawn of industrialized agriculture. I feel strongly that it is both our obligation and our privilege to actively explore what the meaning of that sharing- and community-focused life was in order to regain a little of its dignity.

Because our dinners bring together dozens of strangers for a single afternoon, the participants are invited to share something of themselves from the start. One of the ways we do this is a ritual we've dubbed the Tradition of the Plates: We ask every guest to bring a dinner plate from his or her home. The dozens of individual plates set down the length of the table effect an incredibly striking visual testament to the diverse community we create every time we set up that table.

After almost a decade of Outstanding in the Field dinners, I have tried to capture on these pages what we do on tour so I can share it with an even larger community. The recipes here are either directly from or similar to dishes we've served at our dinners. Some ingredients may seem unusual, and you'll notice an emphasis on specific varieties of fruits and vegetables. Wherever possible I give substitutions, as, of course, not everything is always available to everyone—and not everyone lives in California. In a few cases I do not offer alternatives, for although I am eager for as many people to try as many of my recipes as possible, sometimes food truly is about a time and a place, and a recipe can tell the story of that time and place as well as or better than any words. The Salad of Santa Rosa Plums, Red Cabbage, Purslane, and Sunflower Petals (page 51), for example, really cannot be made with anything besides purslane and sunflower petals, so it is definitely a height-of-summer dish. It is not my goal to be

doctrinaire or obsessive with the recipes in this book. I'm not suggesting that if you live in Maine you should never buy oranges. You'll notice my pantry is full of ingredients that require shipment across the country or even the world: Capers, anchovies, tomato paste, and lemons are staples in my cooking, and they are all available year-round. The goal is to build a tasty, satisfying meal primarily with what is local and seasonal, supplementing with ingredients from farther afield. The reality is that it's tricky to eat strictly locally and seasonally all the time, but that doesn't mean we shouldn't try to find a good deal of our foods from close to home when possible. There are an increasing number of ways to do this: Purchase local chickens at a farmers' market instead of industrial ones shipped cross-country and enjoy domestic berries from late spring to early fall instead of buying imported berries in January, for example. Throughout this book, I talk about resources to help you find out what grows in your region and how you can get your hands on it. In addition, there's a full listing of all these resources at the back of the book (page 246). And more and more, even national chain supermarkets are indicating where their produce originates so you can make these decisions at the point of purchase.

In the end, it all comes down to this: I, like you, enjoy food that is interesting and tasty. So please, grab your plate, pull up a chair, and join me on a journey from farm to table.

appetizers

TOMATO WATER

———

RADISHES WITH ANCHOVY BUTTER

———

GOAT CHEESE CROSTINI WITH SWEET PEA PESTO

———

SAVORY PECAN, PARMESAN, AND THYME SHORTBREAD

———

CHICKEN LIVER PÂTÉ

———

BRAISED BROCCOLI RABE AND CHEESE BRUSCHETTA

———

FRESH MARINATED ANCHOVIES AND PARSLEY SALAD ON CROSTINI

———

GRILLED SQUID WITH CORN, CHERRY TOMATOES, AND MARJORAM

———

BAKED EGGS WITH SPINACH AND CREAM

———

FRIED SQUASH BLOSSOMS FILLED WITH LAVENDER RICOTTA

———

SALTED COD AND POTATO CROQUETTES

tomato water

SERVES 18 TO 24

3 pounds very ripe tomatoes
Kosher salt

The title of this recipe is not an exaggeration: Perfectly ripe tomatoes produce an elixir as clear as water, bursting with concentrated, pure tomato flavor. It's an ideal recipe to make at the peak of tomato season, when flavorful tomatoes are abundant at farmers' markets and in backyard gardens. The number of servings will vary tremendously depending on the variety of tomato you use. Figure about six to eight 1-ounce servings per pound of tomatoes. The pulp that remains after the juice is strained off doesn't have much flavor left so it's best to discard it in the compost pile. I used Early Girl tomatoes to make this appetizer at a dinner to benefit Alice Waters's Chez Panisse Foundation held under the trees of an organic peach orchard at Frog Hollow Farm in Brentwood, California. Tomato water also makes a refreshing break between courses of a summertime meal.

LINE A LARGE STRAINER or colander with several layers of cheesecloth and set it over a large bowl.

Coarsely chop the tomatoes and transfer them to the bowl of a food processor. Add a large pinch of salt, and process until puréed.

Pour the tomato purée into the strainer and let drain slowly overnight in the refrigerator. Taste and adjust the seasoning. Pour into chilled shot glasses and serve.

radishes with anchovy butter

12 small radishes, greens still attached

6 anchovy fillets

3 tablespoons unsalted butter, softened

SERVES 4 TO 6

Eat the peppery radish greens right along with the pink or white bulbs. Although it is best to serve these beautiful little bites as soon after preparing them as possible, when the greens are very crisp, if you need to prepare them ahead of time you can cover the platter with a damp cloth and place it in the refrigerator for up to 1 hour. Let stand at room temperature for 10 minutes before serving.

CLEAN THE RADISHES, removing any dirt and any less than perfect greens. Trim the roots. Cut the radishes in half, leaving some leaves attached to each side.

Pound the anchovies in a mortar and pestle until smooth, or mash with a fork. Add the butter and work it into the anchovies until well combined.

Using a butter knife, spread the anchovy butter on the cut side of each radish. Arrange the radishes on a platter and serve.

goat cheese crostini with sweet pea pesto

When spring is in full swing, there is no substitute for fresh peas in pods. These pretty crostini show them off to best advantage, highlighting their sweetness with toasted nuts, tangy goat cheese, and fresh herbs. Choose pods that are plump but not puffy, brightly colored, and not at all shriveled or blemished. It's important that the peas are cooked until tender enough to pound into a paste. The cooking time will vary depending on how old the peas are. Taste one before draining them all to be sure.

2 tablespoons pine nuts

1 cup shelled fresh sweet English peas (from 12 ounces to 1 pound peas in the pod)

1 small clove garlic

2 tablespoons packed fresh flat-leaf parsley leaves

2 tablespoons packed fresh chervil leaves

About 4 tablespoons extra-virgin olive oil, plus more for serving

Kosher salt and freshly ground black pepper

1 baguette

5 ounces soft, fresh goat cheese

HEAT THE OVEN to 400°F.

Spread the pine nuts on a baking sheet and toast in the oven until golden, 3 to 5 minutes. Transfer the nuts to a plate and set aside to cool.

Increase the oven temperature to 425°F.

Bring a pot of salted water to a boil and prepare a bowl of ice water. Cook the peas in the boiling water until very tender but still bright green, 2 to 6 minutes. Drain the peas and immediately transfer them to the ice water to stop the cooking. When they are cool, drain and dry them on a towel.

In a mortar, use a pestle to pound the garlic clove with a pinch of salt to a paste. Add the peas and pound into a paste, adding a little olive oil to help if necessary. Transfer the mixture to a medium bowl. Add the pine nuts to the mortar and pound them briefly to break them up, but do not pound them to a paste; they should still have a bit of texture. Add the nuts to the pea mixture. Coarsely chop the parsley and chervil and add them to the bowl. Stir in enough olive oil to loosen the pesto but not enough to make it runny. Season with salt and pepper to taste and set aside.

Slice the baguette into ¼-inch slices. Arrange the slices on a baking sheet, and toast in the hot oven until golden, 6 to 8 minutes. Cool slightly.

Spread about ½ teaspoon of the goat cheese on each crostini and grind some black pepper over the cheese. Arrange the crostini on a platter and top each with about 1 teaspoon of the pesto. Drizzle with some olive oil and serve.

savory pecan, parmesan, and thyme shortbread

½ cup pecans

½ cup unsalted butter, room temperature

½ cup freshly grated Parmesan cheese

1 cup unbleached all-purpose flour

1 tablespoon chopped fresh thyme leaves

½ teaspoon kosher salt

¼ teaspoon freshly ground pepper

MAKES ABOUT 3 DOZEN SHORTBREAD COOKIES; SERVES 6 TO 8

We rolled up in our bus for a September dinner at Boggy Creek Farm (page 197) in Austin, Texas, just as a late-summer storm hit, and we quickly found shelter under the beautiful old pecan trees that dot the property. It would have been lovely to have these little savory pecan shortbread cookies on the bus while we waited for that storm to pass. These are fantastic with a dry sparkling wine just before dinner. They are a breeze for the host because most of the work can be done in advance. Roll and chill the dough logs, and then slice and bake the shortbread just before your guests arrive, filling the kitchen with the aroma of toasted nuts and cheese.

HEAT THE OVEN to 375°F.

Spread the pecans on a baking sheet and toast in the oven until fragrant, about 8 minutes. Transfer to a plate to cool. Chop coarsely.

Put the butter in the bowl of an electric mixer and beat on medium speed until fluffy and light. Add the Parmesan and beat on medium until well blended. Remove the bowl from the mixer and stir in the flour, toasted pecans, thyme, salt, and pepper, first with a wooden spoon and then continuing with your hands just until the dough comes together. Roll the dough into two 1½- to 2-inch-wide logs and wrap them in plastic wrap. Refrigerate for at least 1 hour or up to 3 days.

Reduce the oven heat to 350°F. Line a baking sheet with parchment paper.

Cut the shortbread into ¼-inch slices and arrange 1 inch apart on the baking sheet. Bake until golden, about 20 minutes. Use a spatula to transfer the shortbread to wire racks to cool.

chicken liver pâté

8 ounces chicken livers

1 tablespoon extra-virgin olive oil

1 tablespoon unsalted butter

1 small red onion, minced

Kosher salt

4 anchovy fillets, coarsely chopped

1 tablespoon capers, drained and
  coarsely chopped

¼ teaspoon crushed red pepper
  flakes

1 tablespoon tomato paste

Freshly ground black pepper

1 to 2 teaspoons chopped fresh
  flat-leaf parsley leaves

Toasted baguette slices or
  crackers, for serving

MAKES 1½ CUPS

Pasture-raised chickens roam freely among the Pinot Noir grapes at Mark Pasternak's Devil's Gulch Ranch in Marin County, California. His poultry is some of the most flavorful I've ever eaten, and it inspired this chicken liver spread.

The pâté can be eaten immediately, but if you have some time, the flavors will mellow and meld if it is refrigerated for a few hours or even overnight before serving. Let it stand at room temperature at least 30 minutes before serving, and then sprinkle with some chopped fresh parsley leaves. Humble parsley is one of my favorite ingredients, and we use it a lot in the field. It adds color, of course, and an especially welcome, bright flavor to savory meat dishes. Try this pâté with a Pinot like the great ones made from Mark's grapes, which we enjoyed at a dinner on his ranch.

TRIM AND DISCARD the connective tissue and any fat between the lobes of the livers. Set aside.

In a medium skillet, heat the oil and butter over low heat until the butter starts to foam. Add the onion with a pinch of salt and cook, stirring frequently, until very soft and fragrant, about 10 minutes.

Move the onion to one side of the pan and add the anchovies, capers, and red pepper flakes to the other side. Cook, stirring, until the anchovies begin to break down, about 2 minutes.

Add the tomato paste to the pan and stir everything together. Cook, stirring frequently, until the tomato paste caramelizes and becomes sweet, about 3 minutes. Season the chicken livers with salt and black pepper and add to the pan. Raise the heat to medium-high and cook, stirring frequently, until the livers are opaque all over and cooked medium-rare to medium, 3 to 4 minutes.

Remove the mixture from the pan and let cool. Roughly chop the livers and vegetables by hand with a sharp knife. (Alternatively, you may use a food processor, pulsing until the mixture is a coarse paste, but the texture is best if the mixture is chopped by hand.) The paste should have a spreadable consistency. Taste and adjust the seasoning with salt and pepper as needed. Serve immediately or cover and refrigerate for up to 1 day. Bring to room temperature before serving.

When ready to serve, transfer to a small bowl and sprinkle the fresh parsley on top. Serve with toasted baguette slices or crackers.

braised broccoli rabe and cheese bruschetta

SERVES 4

Bruschetta is a good starter for a meal prepared on the grill. If a grill is not available, however, you can still get excellent results using a stovetop grill pan. Let the bread get dark in spots for good, smoky, caramelized flavor. Some people find broccoli rabe's bitterness overly assertive, but slow cooking mellows its sharpness. These also make good brunch or lunch fare.

1 large bunch broccoli rabe (about 1 pound)

2 cloves garlic

2 tablespoons extra-virgin olive oil, plus more for serving

4 anchovy fillets, chopped

1 small dried red chile, minced, or ½ teaspoon crushed red pepper flakes

Kosher salt

½ cup Chicken Stock (page 208) or low-sodium broth

1 tablespoon vinegar, any type (optional)

4 slices country bread, each ½ inch thick

4 ounces fontina, gruyère, or a semi-hard sheep's milk cheese, thinly sliced

Freshly ground black pepper

REMOVE AND DISCARD any tough stems from the broccoli rabe and chop the remaining vegetable finely. Mince 1 clove garlic; peel and set aside the second clove.

In a heavy-bottomed skillet, heat the olive oil over medium-low heat to hot but not smoking. Add the minced garlic, anchovy, and chile, and cook, stirring, until the garlic is fragrant and the anchovy has melted, about 1 minute. Add the broccoli rabe and a pinch of salt. Cook, stirring frequently, until the broccoli rabe begins to give off a little moisture, 1 to 2 minutes. Add a few tablespoons of the chicken stock and cook, adding more of the chicken stock whenever the pan is dry, until the broccoli rabe is tender, 10 to 12 minutes.

Toast the slices of bread over hot coals or on a stovetop grill pan over medium-high heat. The edges can be slightly burned and caramelized.

Rub the toast with the peeled garlic, and drizzle generously with olive oil. Divide the broccoli rabe among the bruschetta and top each with a few slices of cheese. Place the bruschetta back on the grill or grill pan over medium-high heat. Cover and cook just until the cheese has melted, 1 to 2 minutes. Divide the bruschetta among 4 plates, drizzle with more olive oil, and season with salt and pepper. Serve immediately.

fresh marinated anchovies and parsley salad on crostini

SERVES 6 TO 8

Always eager to use the freshest ingredients possible, for a dinner at Route One Farm near Santa Cruz, Katherine Stern, my sous chef at Gabriella Café, and I trekked to the municipal wharf and dropped our lines into a huge cloud of anchovies. If you are not near anchovy waters and cannot find the fish in your area, substitute an equal weight of sardines.

1 pound fresh Monterey Bay or
   other anchovies (20 to 40)
2 to 3 tablespoons kosher salt
10 fresh thyme sprigs
1 lemon
Extra-virgin olive oil
1 baguette
1 cup fresh flat-leaf parsley leaves
2 tablespoons capers, drained
1 small shallot, sliced into thin
   rounds

HOLDING AN ANCHOVY belly side up, pinch its head between your thumb and forefinger and pull it toward the tail, removing the head and guts with one pull. Lay it on a cutting board and cut off its tail with a sharp knife, then spread it open and use your fingers or the tip of the knife to lift the spine up and out of the body. If necessary, cut to separate the two fillets. Repeat with the remaining anchovies.

Lay the fillets in a 2-inch-deep tray in a single layer. Sprinkle with an even layer of the salt and scatter a few of the thyme sprigs on top. Remove the zest from the lemon with a vegetable peeler; set the lemon aside. Place a few strips of zest over the anchovies. Drizzle with olive oil. Repeat with another layer until all of the anchovies are used. Scatter the remaining thyme sprigs and lemon zest on top. Cover the fish with plastic wrap, and then top with another pan that fits easily inside. Place a couple of cans or other weights inside the empty pan and refrigerate overnight.

Heat the oven to 400°F.

Cut the baguette on a slant into ½-inch-thick slices. Spread out on a baking sheet and toast in the oven until golden and crisp, about 8 minutes. Set the crostini aside to cool.

Combine the parsley, capers, and shallot in a small bowl. Squeeze the juice from the lemon into the bowl and add olive oil, salt, and pepper to taste.

Lay 1 or 2 anchovy fillets on each crostini. Top with the parsley salad and another drizzle of olive oil, if desired, before serving.

grilled squid with corn, cherry tomatoes, and marjoram

SERVES 4

Corn, cherry tomatoes, marjoram, and even squid all have a degree of natural sweetness that is enhanced in this dish by the way each is cooked. The combination of smoky-sweet flavors and vibrant colors makes a tantalizing first course.

SEE PHOTOGRAPH ON PAGE 18.

4 ears sweet corn

4 sprigs fresh marjoram

2 tablespoons extra-virgin olive oil,
    plus more for serving

1 tablespoon unsalted butter

1 shallot, chopped

Kosher salt and freshly ground
    black pepper

1 pint cherry tomatoes, halved

12 ounces cleaned squid bodies
    and tentacles

PREPARE a medium-hot grill. The coals should be ashed over, with no visible flames.

While the grill is heating, prepare the corn and tomato mixture. Use a sharp knife to cut the kernels from the ears, scraping and saving any of the liquid from the cobs with the kernels. Strip the marjoram leaves from the stems, reserving the stems for another use.

In a large skillet, heat 1 tablespoon of the olive oil and the butter over low heat. Add the shallot with a pinch of salt and cook, stirring occasionally, until soft and golden, about 8 minutes. Add the corn and its liquid, the marjoram leaves, and salt and pepper to taste. Raise the heat to high and cook, stirring frequently, about 2 minutes. Add the tomatoes and cook just until they are warm but do not break down, 1 to 2 minutes. Remove from the heat and keep warm.

Season the squid with salt and pepper and toss with the remaining 1 tablespoon olive oil. Grill over the hot coals, turning once or twice, until the squid is opaque and shows a few grill marks, 2 to 3 minutes total. Avoid overcooking, as the squid will become tough.

Divide the corn and tomato mixture among 4 warmed plates. Top each with grilled squid and a drizzle of olive oil and serve.

baked eggs with spinach and cream

SERVES 4

Tangy spinach is complemented here by velvety eggs and cream. An excellent first course, this dish is also fine for brunch or lunch; serve with good bread.

1 tablespoon unsalted butter, plus
    more for greasing the dishes
2 pounds fresh spinach, stemmed
    and cleaned
Kosher salt
1 clove garlic
¾ cup heavy cream
Freshly ground black pepper
4 large eggs

HEAT THE OVEN to 400°F. Butter the bottom and sides of four 8-ounce, ovenproof dishes or ramekins. Arrange the dishes on a rimmed baking sheet and set aside.

In a large, wide skillet, melt 1 tablespoon butter over medium-high heat. When the foaming subsides, add the spinach and a pinch of salt. You may need to add the spinach in a few batches and use tongs to turn it over a few times until it is wilted enough to make room for the rest of the spinach. Cook, stirring occasionally, until the leaves are completely wilted, about 2 minutes. Pour off all the liquid in the skillet.

Using the side of a knife, crush the garlic and add it to the spinach along with the cream. Gently simmer the mixture, stiming occasionally, until the cream has reduced slightly, 3 to 4 minutes. Remove the garlic and season the spinach with salt and pepper.

Divide the spinach mixture among the dishes and make a small well in the center of each. Crack an egg into the well in the spinach in each of the dishes. Bake the dishes on the baking sheet until the white is set but the yolk is still runny, 12 to 15 minutes.

Season with salt and pepper and serve immediately.

fried squash blossoms filled with lavender ricotta

1½ cups fresh whole-milk ricotta
  cheese
12 large, fresh, male squash
  blossoms
1 teaspoon active dry yeast
¼ cup warm water
1 cup unbleached all-purpose flour
Kosher salt
1 cup ice water
Vegetable oil, for deep-frying
1 tablespoon fresh lavender buds or
  thyme leaves
¼ cup freshly grated Parmesan
  cheese
Freshly ground black pepper

SERVES 4 TO 6

Fresh squash blossoms, which come most often from zucchini plants, are such a treat in part because they're so fleeting. They do not store longer than a day or so, thus it is the rare supermarket that will carry them. They are the treasures of the home garden and farmers' market. Male blossoms are thinner and less bulb shaped than female blossoms and grow at the end of stems. Female blossoms grow at the end of the squash itself and are not as desirable for this recipe.

SPOON THE RICOTTA into the center of a large piece of doubled-over cheesecloth and tie the ends together tightly with butcher's twine. Tie the bundle to the handle of a wooden spoon and lay the spoon across the top of a bowl deep enough that the ricotta bundle does not touch the bottom. Refrigerate overnight.

Carefully pinch off the stamen from inside each of the squash blossoms. Trim the stems, leaving about 2 inches of stem on each blossom. Set the blossoms aside.

Combine the yeast and warm water in a small bowl and let sit until foamy, about 10 minutes. Put the flour and a pinch of salt in a medium bowl and slowly whisk in the yeast mixture and then the ice water to make a smooth batter. Pour the batter through a finemesh strainer into another bowl to remove any lumps. Set aside for 20 minutes.

Meanwhile, pour oil into a large, deep pot, such as a Dutch oven, so that it is at least 2½ inches deep but comes no more than halfway up the sides of the pot. Attach a candy or deep-frying thermometer to the side of the pot. Heat the oil over medium heat to 375°F.

While the oil is heating, squeeze the ricotta bundle firmly to force out all the liquid. The ricotta should be very dry; if you form a tablespoonful into a ball, it should hold its shape. Put the drained ricotta in a bowl. Gently bruise the lavender buds or thyme leaves with a mortar and pestle, or coarsely chop them with a knife. Add them to the ricotta along with the Parmesan and stir to combine. Season to taste with salt and pepper.

Fill each squash blossom with about 1 teaspoon of the ricotta mixture and gently twist the top so no filling will come out when frying.

Holding a blossom by the stem, dip it into the batter and let the excess run off. Then carefully add it to the hot oil. Fry just a few at a time until golden brown and crisp, about 1 minute. Drain on paper towels and serve immediately, sprinkled with salt, if desired.

salted cod and potato croquettes

1 pound salt cod
8 ounces all-purpose potatoes,
    such as russet, Yukon Gold, or
    Kennebec varieties
Kosher salt
2 tablespoons olive oil
1 small onion, minced
1 tablespoon chopped fresh flat-leaf
    parsley leaves
2 teaspoons finely chopped fresh
    chives
4 large eggs
Freshly ground black pepper
1 cup unbleached all-purpose flour
2½ cups fresh white bread crumbs
    (from about 5 cups cubed
    crustless bread)
Vegetable oil, for deep-frying
Lemon Mayonnaise (page 206)

At Quail Hill Farm in Amagansett, on Long Island, New York, the Yukon Gold potatoes thrive in the fertile glacial soil. Matched with salt cod and enrobed in a crispy crust, these croquettes are bursting with potato and salty fish flavor. They are excellent with a crisp white wine, such as a Long Island Sauvignon Blanc.

PUT THE SALT COD in a large bowl or deep pan and cover it with cold water. Place the bowl in the refrigerator and leave the cod to soak for 12 hours. Drain the fish and cover with fresh cold water. Return to the refrigerator for an additional 12 hours. Remove the fish from the water and pat it dry on a towel. Cut into strips about 1 inch thick. Set aside.

Wash and peel the potatoes and cut them into large cubes. Put the potatoes in a pot, cover with cold water, and season the water with 1 teaspoon salt. Bring to a boil over high heat, then reduce the heat and simmer until the potatoes are tender when pierced with a knife, about 30 minutes. Drain well. While still warm, pass the potatoes through a ricer or food mill into a large bowl and set aside.

In a large skillet, heat the olive oil over medium-low heat until hot but not smoking. Add the onion with a pinch of salt and cook, stirring occasionally, until soft but not browned, about 8 minutes. Lay the pieces of fish on top of the onions and cook over low heat, turning periodically, until the fish begins to flake, 10 to 15 minutes.

Use a slotted spoon to transfer the fish to a bowl, straining off any juices. Add the minced onion to the bowl with the fish. Using a fork, flake the fish into small pieces.

Add the flaked fish and onions to the potato along with the parsley, chives, and 1 of the eggs, season with salt and pepper and stir to combine. Cover the mixture and refrigerate for 1 hour.

Pour the oil into a large, deep pot, such as a Dutch oven, so that it is at least 2½ inches deep but comes no more than halfway up the sides of the pot. Attach a candy or deep-frying thermometer to the side of the pot and heat the oil over medium heat to 375°F.

While the oil is heating, put the flour in a shallow dish and season with salt and pepper. Beat the remaining 3 eggs in another shallow dish. Place the bread crumbs in a third shallow dish. Remove the potato mixture from the refrigerator and roll it between your hands into 1½-inch balls. Roll each ball in the flour, then dip it in the egg, and then coat it in bread crumbs. Set aside the breaded croquettes on a plate.

Using a mesh skimmer to move the croquettes in and out of the hot oil, fry 4 croquettes at a time until golden brown, 1 to 1½ minutes. Drain on paper towels.

Arrange the croquettes on a platter and serve warm with the mayonnaise.

salads

LITTLE GEM LETTUCE WITH CHOPPED EGG AND LEMON

———

LEMON CUCUMBERS WITH OREGANO, FETA, AND PINE NUTS

———

WILTED DANDELION SALAD WITH PANCETTA AND POACHED EGG

———

BURRATA CHEESE WITH NECTARINES, MÂCHE, AND HAZELNUTS

———

FRESH SHELL BEAN AND HERB SALAD

———

CARAMELIZED CARROT SALAD

———

BUTTER LETTUCE WITH SEARED CHICKEN LIVERS AND RADISHES

———

HARICOT VERT AND EARLY GIRL TOMATO SALAD WITH SUMMER SAVORY

———

SALAD OF SANTA ROSA PLUMS, RED CABBAGE, PURSLANE, AND SUNFLOWER PETALS

———

BREAD SALAD WITH PEPPERS, RADICCHIO, AND BLACK OLIVES

———

POTATO, SWEET CHILE, AND WILD FENNEL SALAD

little gem lettuce with chopped egg and lemon

6 heads of Little Gem lettuce

4 large eggs

1 lemon

6 anchovy fillets

½ cup extra-virgin olive oil

Freshly ground black pepper
  (optional)

SERVES 4 TO 6

Little Gem is a variety of Cos lettuce that grows only about 5 inches tall (see photograph on page 36). Flavorful Little Gem is a lot like a cross between crunchy, assertive romaine (another Cos lettuce) and tender, sweet butterhead lettuce. It is well worth seeking out for this salad, or try it in any other favorite salad in which you normally use either romaine or butterhead lettuces. If you absolutely can't find Little Gem, use heads of baby romaine or butterhead in its place.

CLEAN THE LETTUCES, removing the core and separating the leaves; include the inner young leaves, as they are very sweet. Wash well and then spin in a salad spinner to dry.

Put the eggs in a single layer in a saucepan and add cold water to cover. Bring to a boil over medium-high heat, then remove from the heat, cover the pan and let sit for 5 minutes. Drain the eggs and fill the pan with ice water. When the eggs are cool, drain well. Peel the eggs and chop them coarsely.

Using a vegetable peeler, remove half the zest from the lemon and chop it finely. Juice the lemon. Put the anchovy fillets in a mortar and pestle and pound to a paste. Add the zest and the lemon juice. Whisking constantly, pour in the oil in a slow, steady stream until emulsified.

Toss the Little Gem leaves with the dressing. Arrange on 4 chilled plates and top with the chopped egg. Grind a little black pepper over the dish, if desired.

lemon cucumbers with oregano, feta, and pine nuts

2 tablespoons pine nuts
½ shallot
2 tablespoons red wine vinegar
8 lemon cucumbers
3 sprigs fresh oregano
¼ cup extra-virgin olive oil
Kosher salt
¼ cup crumbled feta (about
    1 ounce)
Freshly ground black pepper

SERVES 4

Sweet lemon cucumbers grow at UBC Farm, which is both a working and teaching farm at the University of British Columbia in Vancouver, Canada. Lemon cucumbers are less sharp than most other cucumbers and they make a refreshing appetizer before a summery main course such as Grilled Squab with Sweet and Sour Cherries and Watercress (page 158), or can be served as a side salad with grilled meat or poultry.

HEAT THE OVEN to 400°F.

Spread the pine nuts on a baking sheet and toast in the oven until golden, 3 to 5 minutes. Transfer the nuts to a plate and set aside to cool. Mince the shallot and combine with the vinegar in a small bowl. Set aside to macerate for about 10 minutes.

Peel the cucumbers and cut them in half lengthwise. Scoop out and discard the seeds. Cut the cucumbers crosswise at a slant into slices ¼ inch thick. You should have about 4 cups. Put the cucumbers in a medium bowl. Strip the oregano leaves from the stems and toss the leaves with the cucumbers.

Whisking constantly, pour the olive oil into the shallot mixture in a slow, steady stream until all of it has been added and the vinaigrette is combined. Season with salt. Pour the vinaigrette over the cucumbers and toss well.

Divide the cucumbers among 4 chilled small plates. Sprinkle with the crumbled feta and then the pine nuts. Grind some pepper on top and serve.

wilted dandelion salad with pancetta and poached egg

SERVES 4

Kosher salt

1 tablespoon vinegar, any kind
  (optional)

2 bunches tender young red or
  white dandelion greens
  (1½ pounds)

1 teaspoon minced shallot

1 tablespoon champagne vinegar

1 teaspoon Dijon mustard

2 tablespoons extra-virgin olive oil

¼ cup diced pancetta (about
  1 ounce)

4 large eggs

Freshly ground black pepper

Bitter greens are set off by crackling pancetta and velvety egg yolk in this dish, which can be served as a starter or on its own for lunch. For best results, use tender young greens, which are less bitter than their older counterparts, and the freshest eggs you can find, as they hold together better when poached. Because it's not always possible to obtain farm-fresh eggs, or even to know exactly how old your eggs are, add a bit of vinegar to the poaching liquid to help eggs of any age stay compact while cooking.

FILL A WIDE, shallow pan with water to about 3 inches deep and add ½ teaspoon salt and the vinegar, if desired. Bring to a low simmer over low heat.

Meanwhile, wash the dandelion greens, removing any tough lower stems. Cut into 1-inch pieces. Set aside.

To make the dressing, put the minced shallot in a small bowl and add the champagne vinegar. Let stand for a few minutes to macerate. Whisk in the mustard and a pinch of salt. Slowly add the oil in a steady stream, whisking constantly until incorporated.

Heat a large, heavy-bottomed skillet over low heat and add the pancetta. Cook until the pancetta is crisp, 6 to 8 minutes. Using a slotted spoon, remove the pancetta from the pan and set aside. Reserve 1 tablespoon fat in the pan.

When the water has reached a very gentle simmer, crack the eggs, one at a time, into the water. This may be easier if you first crack each egg into a small cup with a handle and then add it to the simmering water. Let the eggs simmer very gently until the whites are just set and the yolks are still soft and runny, about 3 minutes.

While the eggs are poaching, place the pancetta pan over high heat. Add the dandelion greens. Cook quickly just to wilt, being careful not to cook the greens so much that they lose their shape and bite, about 2 minutes. Remove the pan from the heat, pour the dressing over the greens, and toss quickly.

Divide the greens among 4 warmed plates and top with the pancetta. Using a slotted spoon, remove the eggs from the poaching water, letting as much water as possible run off. Place an egg on top of each salad. Grind a bit of black pepper on top of each egg and serve immediately.

burrata cheese with nectarines, mâche, and hazelnuts

SERVES 6

Burrata is an extraordinary cheese; a thin sheath of mozzarella stretches to enclose a velvety center of ricotta-like cream and mozzarella threads. It is best served at cool room temperature—do not let it get too warm, or you'll have an oozy mess on your hands. Here sweet nectarines, nutty mâche, and fruity olive oil underscore the burrata's creamy yet tangy delicateness. Third-generation cheesemaker Vito Girardi of Gioia makes the best-known domestic burrata at his cheese dairy in West Los Angeles. He provided the burrata for our dinner at Coleman Farm in Carpinteria, California.

¼ cup shelled hazelnuts

2 ripe nectarines

3 to 4 ounces mâche

8 ounces burrata cheese (1 small or 2 large balls), at room temperature

Kosher salt and freshly ground black pepper

2 tablespoons extra-virgin olive oil

PREHEAT THE OVEN to 400°F.

Spread the hazelnuts on a baking sheet and toast in the oven until they are fragrant and their skins loosen, 5 to 7 minutes. Transfer the hazelnuts to a plate and let cool slightly. Rub the hazelnuts in a folded kitchen towel to release their skins. Coarsely chop the nuts and set aside.

Cut the nectarines in half and remove the pits. Slice the fruits into thin wedges. Wash the mâche in a sink filled with cold water. Carefully remove any dirt or sand stuck between the leaves and discard any root ends. Dry the mâche in a salad spinner.

Cut the burrata into ¼-inch slices; because it is very soft, it might be easier to slice with a serrated knife. Arrange the cheese on 6 chilled salad plates. Season with salt and freshly ground pepper and drizzle with 1 tablespoon of the olive oil.

In a medium bowl, toss together the mâche and the nectarines with the remaining olive oil. Season with salt. Arrange on top of the burrata. Sprinkle with the hazelnuts and serve.

fresh shell bean and herb salad

SERVES 4 TO 6

3 cups shelled fresh beans such as cranberry, flageolet, or cannelloni (from about 3 pounds in the pods)

1 small onion, peeled and halved

1 carrot, peeled and cut in half

1 rib celery, cut in half

2 fresh or dried bay leaves

Kosher salt

1 tablespoon minced shallot

¼ cup fresh lemon juice

¾ cup extra-virgin olive oil

¼ cup chopped fresh flat-leaf parsley leaves

3 tablespoons chopped fresh chervil leaves

2 tablespoons chopped fresh chives

1 tablespoon chopped fresh marjoram leaves

Freshly ground black pepper

I made this salad on a warm afternoon in late summer for one of our dinners at Zephyros Farm in Paonia, Colorado, set in a valley below scenic Lamborn Peak. Zephyros farmers Don Lareau and Daphne Yannakakis grow dragon's lingerie beans, one of many different fresh shell beans that may be used in this salad. It is great with grilled meats at a barbecue or as a side dish for a summer picnic.

COMBINE THE BEANS, onion, carrot, celery, and bay leaves in a large pot and cover with cold water. Bring to a boil and then reduce the heat so that the mixture simmers. Cook until the beans are tender, 30 to 45 minutes, depending on their size. Remove the pot from the heat and add about 1½ teaspoons salt and some black pepper to the cooking liquid; the liquid should taste like salty seawater. Allow the beans to cool in their liquid.

To make the dressing, combine the shallot and the lemon juice in a small bowl and let stand for 10 minutes. Add a pinch of salt and then whisk in the olive oil in a slow, steady stream.

Drain the beans, removing the vegetables and bay leaves. Put the beans in a large bowl and add the parsley, chervil, chives, and marjoram. Add the dressing and mix well to combine. Taste the salad and adjust the seasoning with salt and pepper as needed. If the salad is too dry, add olive oil to moisten. Serve at room temperature.

caramelized carrot salad

SERVES 4 TO 6

Use the sweetest carrots you can find for this preparation, which draws out and highlights the vegetable's natural sweetness. The dish is especially beautiful when the familiar orange carrots are mixed with colorful varieties, such as maroon Purple Dragons or Red Indians, light yellow Yellowstones, and white Snow Whites. If using colorful varieties, scrub them well under running water, but don't peel them, as you'll take off a lot of their glorious color with the peel. This salad may be served hot or cold and is great with fish or roasted meats.

SEE PHOTOGRAPH ON PAGE 187.

½ cup pine nuts

3 pounds carrots, preferably a mix of orange, maroon, light yellow, and white

About ¾ cup extra-virgin olive oil

1 large shallot, minced

¼ cup fresh lemon juice

2 tablespoons minced preserved lemon peel (page 205)

2 tablespoons chopped fresh flat-leaf parsley leaves

2 tablespoons chopped fresh mint leaves

Freshly ground black pepper

HEAT THE OVEN to 400°F.

Spread the pine nuts on a baking sheet and toast in the oven until golden, 3 to 5 minutes. Transfer the nuts to a plate and set aside to cool.

Slice the carrots on a slant into thin ovals. Heat 1 tablespoon of the olive oil in a heavy-bottomed skillet over medium heat. Add about one-quarter of the carrots to the pan and allow them to caramelize and brown, stirring only occasionally. This should take 10 to 15 minutes. Transfer the carrots to a plate lined with paper towels in order to drain off any excess oil. Season with salt. Wipe out the pan and add another tablespoon of the olive oil. Cook the remaining carrots in batches in the same manner.

Mix together the shallot and the lemon juice and set aside to macerate for 10 minutes. Add a pinch of salt and slowly pour in ½ cup olive oil, whisking constantly until the dressing is well combined.

In a medium bowl, combine the carrots, pine nuts, preserved lemon peel, parsley, and mint. Pour the dressing into the bowl and toss to combine. Season with salt and pepper before serving.

butter lettuce with seared chicken livers and radishes

SERVES 4

The soft, flavorful leaves of butter lettuce are a great backdrop for savory seared chicken livers and spicy, crunchy radishes. Banyuls vinegar is made from Banyuls wine, a sweet fortified wine from the Pyrenees in southwestern France. Fortified wines have spirits added to them after the grapes have fermented; other popular fortified wines are Madeira, port, and Marsala. Banyuls vinegar is mellower than regular red wine vinegar and is a good choice for tender, buttery greens. It can be found in well-stocked grocery stores and gourmet food stores.

1 head butter lettuce

1 bunch small red radishes

8 ounces chicken livers

1 tablespoon extra-virgin olive oil, plus more for serving

Kosher salt and freshly ground black pepper

1 small shallot, sliced into thin rounds

3 tablespoons Banyuls vinegar

½ cup Chicken Stock (page 208) or low-sodium broth

TRIM THE BOTTOM from the butter lettuce and separate the leaves. Wash well and spin in a salad spinner to dry. Tear the largest leaves in half. Set aside in a large bowl.

Trim the greens from the radishes and discard or reserve for another use. Using a sharp knife or a mandoline, slice the radishes into thin rounds. Set aside.

Trim and discard the connective tissue and any fat from the livers, dividing them into separate lobes. Season them with salt and pepper.

In a heavy-bottomed skillet, heat the olive oil over medium-high heat until hot but not smoking. Lay the chicken livers in the hot pan and cook for 1 to 2 minutes on each side until opaque and cooked medium-rare to medium; they should be pink to light pink throughout. Set aside to rest on a warm plate.

Add the shallots to the pan and cook, stirring, until golden and soft, about 5 minutes. Add the vinegar and then the chicken stock and boil until reduced by half. Remove the pan from the heat.

Toss the butter lettuce and the radishes together with a splash of olive oil and some salt and pepper. Arrange on 4 plates. Top with the seared chicken livers and spoon the sauce over the livers. Serve.

haricot vert and early girl tomato salad with summer savory

SERVES 4

Flavorful haricots verts have an almost herbal taste that is nicely set off in this salad by juicy, sweet Early Girl tomatoes and a generous amount of summer savory. Early Girls are great for a home garden because they ripen more quickly than other varieties, allowing you to reap early rewards for your work.

1 small shallot, minced

2 tablespoons sherry vinegar

8 ounces haricots verts

1½ pounds Early Girl or other ripe heirloom tomatoes (about 4)

2 sprigs fresh summer savory

1 teaspoon Dijon mustard

Kosher salt

⅓ cup extra-virgin olive oil

Freshly ground black pepper

PUT THE SHALLOT into a small bowl with the vinegar and set aside to macerate for about 10 minutes.

Clean the haricots verts and remove the tops; the tails are fine to leave on. Bring a pot of salted water to a boil and prepare a bowl of ice water. Add the trimmed haricots verts to the boiling water and boil for 1 to 2 minutes, until tender but still firm to the bite (al dente). Drain the beans and plunge them immediately into the ice water to stop the cooking. When cool, remove from the water and dry on a towel. Set aside.

Core the tomatoes and cut them into thin wedges. Strip the leaves off the summer savory sprigs and coarsely chop the leaves.

Add the mustard and a pinch of salt to the shallot and vinegar and whisk together. Whisking constantly, pour in the olive oil in a slow, steady stream until all of it has been added and the vinaigrette is emulsified.

In a large bowl, toss together the haricots verts, tomatoes, and summer savory. Pour the vinaigrette over the top and season with salt to taste. Mix well to coat the vegetables with the vinaigrette. Divide the salad among 4 chilled plates. Grind a bit of black pepper over each and serve, or pass the pepper grinder at the table after serving.

salad of santa rosa plums, red cabbage, purslane, and sunflower petals

SERVES 6

½ head red cabbage

6 ripe Santa Rosa plums

4 ounces purslane, washed

¼ cup fresh lemon basil leaves

¼ cup sunflower petals

Juice of ½ lemon

1 tablespoon extra-virgin olive oil,
    or more to taste

Kosher salt and freshly ground
    black pepper

I prefer to write the menus for Outstanding dinners after I have visited the farm, usually a day or two before the event. I need to see and taste what is there and ready for picking before I decide what to serve. On a pre-dinner visit to Route One Farm near Santa Cruz one year it was hard to miss the towering sunflowers, their full faces leaning toward the sun. Close by I could see trees full of perfectly ripe Santa Rosa plums, just at the height of their short season. Purslane, considered a weed by so many, was flourishing between the rows of plum trees. This remarkable salad is the reflection of what was abundant that memorable day: Sweet and tangy plums, tart purslane, and nutty sunflower petals mingle with beautiful red cabbage. Although many types of sunflowers work for this dish, I recommend "teddy bear" sunflowers, which are mostly petals with a few seeds. Just pinch the petals off the flower; they come right off. Be sure to use unsprayed flowers.

CORE THE CABBAGE. Using a sharp knife or a mandoline, slice the cabbage very thinly and put it in a large bowl.

Cut the plums in half and remove the stones. Slice the fruits into thin wedges and add them to the bowl. If the stones cling too firmly to separate the halves easily, slice into the pit, cutting the plum into thin wedges and lifting each slice out.

Remove and discard the thick stems from the purslane. Place the succulent leaves and the tender tops in the bowl.

Tear any large basil leaves into 1-inch pieces, leaving the small leaves whole. Add the basil to the bowl along with the sunflower petals.

Add the lemon juice and the oil to the bowl and toss gently. Season the salad to taste with salt and pepper. Serve immediately.

bread salad with peppers, radicchio, and black olives

SERVES 6 TO 8

1 loaf country bread, crust
   removed

2 yellow bell peppers

1 pound ripe, juicy tomatoes, such
   as Early Girl or Brandywine

1 medium cucumber

1 head Chioggia radicchio

2 tablespoons capers, drained

½ cup dry cured black olives,
   halved and pitted

2 tablespoons chopped anchovy

3 tablespoons balsamic vinegar

½ cup extra-virgin olive oil

Kosher salt and freshly ground
   black pepper

¼ cup basil leaves

We served this bread salad at one of our first dinners, held at Greg Beccio's Happy Boy Farm in Hollister, California. We had a small number of guests, so we were able to harvest the tomatoes, peppers, and cucumbers ourselves the morning of the dinner. Greg's farm is one of the most remote we've been to, and when we were leaving the farm early the next morning we saw a raccoon, a deer, and a bobcat.

Chioggia radicchio is a rounded head about the size of a grapefruit. The tapered varieties may also be used here.

HEAT THE OVEN to 350°F.

Cut the bread into 1-inch cubes. Arrange the cubes in a single layer on a baking sheet and toast until the bread is dried out all over, about 10 minutes.

Raise the oven temperature to 450°F.

Put the bread cubes in a large bowl and sprinkle 1 or 2 tablespoons warm water on top. Toss and lightly rub the bread cubes with your hands until they are evenly moist all over. Add a few more teaspoons warm water if necessary, but do not add so much water that you can squeeze it out of the bread. Set aside.

Put the peppers on a rimmed baking sheet and roast in the hot oven, turning them over once or twice, until their skins are blistered, 35 to 40 minutes. Transfer the peppers to a bowl and tightly cover the bowl with plastic wrap. Let sit for 10 to 15 minutes before uncovering. When the peppers are cool enough to handle, use a paring knife to remove and discard their skins and seeds. Do not rinse the peppers, or you will wash away some of the roasted flavor. Cut the peppers into 1-inch pieces and set aside.

While the peppers are roasting, cut the tomatoes in half and remove and discard the cores and seeds. Cut them into ½-inch cubes. Peel, halve, and seed the cucumber. Cut crosswise at a slant into ¼-inch slices. Cut the radicchio in half and cut out the core. Slice each half crosswise into thin strips.

In a large bowl, combine the bread, peppers, tomatoes, cucumbers, radicchio, capers, and olives. Toss together until well combined. In a small bowl, whisk together the anchovies, balsamic vinegar, and olive oil, and pour over the bread mixture. Season with salt and pepper to taste and mix well.

Let the salad stand at room temperature for at least 3 hours, or refrigerate it overnight to allow the flavors to intensify. If refrigerated, let the salad stand at room temperature for 1 hour before serving. Immediately before serving, tear the basil leaves into 1-inch pieces and add them to the salad.

Community
Gardens and CSAs

After dozens of dinners in fields and at the edge of the wilderness, we decided it was time for a new challenge: a farm dinner in New York City. This meant both finding a location that qualified as a farm and sourcing enough ingredients grown and produced in or very close to the city to feed 100 people. We found both with the help of Just Food (www.justfood.org), a wonderful organization dedicated to connecting New York City communities with sustainable food sources in and just beyond the city. They led us to an urban field, La Plaza Cultural Community Garden in the East Village in Manhattan, and a number of urban farmers, including Classie Parker, who has gardened at Five Star Garden in Harlem for more than twelve years. As is my habit when we are on tour, the day before our dinner, I set out to walk the fields to see what was ripe and ready for picking and cooking. On my visit to Classie's plot she pointed out her lush collards, abundant basil plants, and her beautiful and prolific pear tree, whose fruit she uses to make the spicy pear preserves that have made her justifiably famous. The next night those luscious preserves were put to good use basting a roasted goat raised on a farm just outside the city. Of course, walking the fields for our urban dinner meant a little more city driving than usual; in addition to the bounty from Classie's plot in Harlem, we used tomatoes from a community garden in Queens, summer squash from another on Staten Island, and honey from Roger Repohl's Bronx bees.

I confess that before this inaugural urban dinner, I was unaware of the bounty growing in many cities across the country. What I have been most struck by since is how very similar these city gardeners are to the more traditional small farmers I've worked with over the years, the kitchen herbs growing through the cracks in the pavement at La Plaza Cultural notwithstanding. Urban gardeners talk with the same passion and detail about varietals, weather challenges, pests, and the health of the soil as do traditional farmers growing the same crops hundreds of miles from the city. The common thread connecting city farmers, rural farmers, and for that matter, anyone else who grows food for themselves and others is a life governed by the seasons and the needs of the earth and crops.

To find out more about turning the earth in your own community garden plot, check out the American Community Gardening Association's website (www.community

garden.org) for information on community gardens in your state. If growing food your-self isn't your thing, another great resource for people inside and outside of cities is Local Harvest (www.localharvest.org), founded by software engineer and activist Guillermo Payet to be a link between consumers and local food sources. Just type in your ZIP code to find all sorts of ways to tap into your local food community, including farms, farmers' markets, restaurants that make sourcing their ingredients locally a pri-ority, food co-ops, and Community Supported Agriculture (CSA). CSA farms offer you the opportunity to buy a share in their harvest before the season begins and receive produce, eggs, flowers, or other products every week or month, usually from late spring

through early fall. Many CSAs also require an often minimal time com-mitment, such as helping bag pro-duce at the delivery site or actually going out and working the fields once or twice. CSAs offer great ben-efits both to the farmer and to you: They provide some income to help subsidize the farmer during the off-season, at a time when there isn't usually much money coming in, and

they provide you with a direct local connection to the source of your food—meaning it's just about as fresh as it can be without your growing it yourself—as well as the sat-isfaction of helping a local farmer. Some CSAs support community garden farmers like those we worked with in New York. True to its name, the Community Supported Agriculture system transforms the small farm into a community endeavor.

potato, sweet chile, and wild fennel salad

SERVES 6 TO 8 AS A SIDE DISH OR APPETIZER

Wild fennel is common in California—just walk out the door and there is probably a patch somewhere—and is often used at our dinners. It is a little stronger and a little chewier than cultivated bulb fennel. If you can't find wild fennel, use instead the fronds from a fennel bulb. You can purchase fennel pollen online or use an equal amount of toasted fennel seed in its place.

2 pounds small, waxy potatoes, such as Russian banana or fingerling

2 pounds fresh sweet chiles, such as Marconi, Figaro, Italia, lipstick, or feherozon

2 tablespoons minced shallot

⅓ cup red wine vinegar

Kosher salt

⅔ cup extra-virgin olive oil

2 tablespoons wild fennel pollen or fennel seed

2 tablespoons chopped young wild fennel fronds or bulb fennel fronds

Freshly ground black pepper

HEAT THE OVEN to 450°F.

Wash the potatoes, place them in a pot, and cover them with cold salted water. Bring to a simmer over medium heat. Reduce the heat to low and simmer uncovered very gently, so the skins do not break, until the potatoes are tender and can be easily pierced with a knife, about 30 minutes. Drain and set aside to cool.

While the potatoes are cooking, put the chiles on a rimmed baking sheet and roast in the oven, turning them over once or twice, until their skins are blistered, 35 to 40 minutes. Transfer the chiles to a bowl and cover with plastic wrap for 10 minutes. Remove the plastic wrap and let the chiles cool. When they are cool enough to handle, remove and discard their skins and seeds with the help of a paring knife and clean kitchen towel. Do not rinse the peppers, or you will wash away some of the roasted flavor. Cut the chiles into ½-inch-wide strips and set aside.

Meanwhile, put the minced shallot in a small bowl and whisk in the vinegar and ½ teaspoon salt. Let stand for 10 minutes. Whisking constantly, pour in the olive oil in a slow, steady stream until all of it has been added and the dressing is combined.

If using the fennel seed, place it in a small cast-iron or other heavy skillet and toast over medium-low heat until fragrant, stirring the seeds or shaking the pan occasionally, about 4 minutes. Let the fennel seeds cool slightly. Transfer them to a mortar and crush the seeds very well with a pestle.

Cut the potatoes in half lengthwise or into 1-inch cubes. In a medium bowl, gently toss the chiles together with the potatoes. Add the dressing, the fennel pollen or crushed fennel seed, and the fennel fronds and mix well. Taste and adjust the seasoning with salt and pepper. Set aside at room temperature for at least 1 hour to incorporate the flavors before serving.

soups

CORN CHOWDER WITH MARJORAM

———

SUMMER VEGETABLE SOUP WITH PISTOU

———

GAZPACHO

———

PUMPKIN AND PERSIMMON SOUP

———

BABY TURNIP SOUP

———

BREAD SOUP WITH BEANS AND KALE

———

CHESTNUT SOUP WITH PORCINI RELISH

———

FARRO SOUP WITH GREENS

corn chowder
with marjoram

SERVES 4

I find the milk or cream usually added to chowders to give them their thick, creamy texture also gives them an unpleasant heaviness and masks the essence of the main ingredient. In this chowder, the corn cob is maximized to draw out every last bit of pure corn flavor. Lush creaminess is achieved by puréeing half the mixture. A dollop of tangy crème fraîche is all the cream this chowder needs.

6 ears sweet corn, husked

3 small onions

2 carrots

1 rib celery

2 fresh or dried bay leaves

1 tablespoon extra-virgin olive oil

2 tablespoons unsalted butter

Kosher salt

1 pound all-purpose potatoes,
    such as Yukon Gold, Kennebec,
    or Yellow Finn

6 sprigs fresh marjoram

Crème fraîche, for serving

HOLD AN EAR OF CORN upright on its end and use a sharp knife to cut off the kernels. Once all of the kernels have been removed, use the knife to scrape all of the juice and remaining bits of kernel from the cobs into a bowl. Repeat with the remaining ears. Set the kernels and juice aside.

Cut the cobs in half and place them in a stockpot. Cut one of the onions into quarters. Cut one of the carrots and the celery into a few large pieces and add them, the quartered onion, and the bay leaves to the stockpot. Cover the contents with cold water and bring to a boil. Reduce the heat so the mixture simmers. Cook until fragrant, about 1 hour. Strain the stock, discarding the solids, and set aside.

Cut the remaining 2 onions and carrot into small dice. In a large heavy-bottomed pot, heat the olive oil and butter over medium-low heat until the butter foams. Add the onions and a pinch of salt. Cook, stirring occasionally, until the onion is soft and translucent, about 8 minutes. Add the carrot and continue to cook, stirring occasionally, until the carrot begins to soften, 7 to 10 minutes.

While the vegetables are cooking, peel the potatoes and cut them into small dice. Strip the leaves off of the marjoram. Add the potatoes, half of the marjoram leaves, the corn and corn juice, and about 1 teaspoon salt to the onions and carrot. Stir to combine and cook for 2 minutes. Add the corn stock to cover and raise the heat to bring the soup to a boil. Reduce the heat and simmer until the potatoes are tender, 20 to 25 minutes, adding stock or water to cover if needed.

Transfer half of the soup to a food processor or blender and purée until smooth. Return the puréed soup to the pot and adjust the consistency with more stock or water as needed. Chop the remaining marjoram leaves. Bring the chowder back to a boil and stir in the marjoram. Ladle into warm bowls and top each serving with a spoonful of crème fraîche. Serve hot.

summer vegetable soup with pistou

SERVES 6

1½ cups fresh cannellini or
  flageolet beans (about
  1½ pounds in the pod) or
  ¾ cup dried beans

1½ onions

1½ carrots

1½ ribs celery

1 sprig fresh thyme

1 bay leaf

Kosher salt

1 tablespoon pine nuts

1 small leek, white and light green
  parts

2 tablespoons plus ⅓ to ½ cup
  extra-virgin olive oil

1 large (about 1 cup) tomato, diced

1 medium summer squash, such as
  zucchini, yellow crookneck, or
  ronde de nice, diced

1 small potato, such as Yellow Finn
  or Yukon Gold, peeled and diced

4 cups Chicken Stock or Vegetable
  Stock (pages 208 or 207) or
  low-sodium broth

8 ounces green beans, such as Blue
  Lake or French fillet, cut into
  1½-inch lengths

1 small clove garlic

1 cup packed fresh basil leaves

Freshly ground black pepper

Pistou is the French Provençal version of the well-known Italian sauce pesto. Both are based on pounded basil, garlic, and olive oil. Pesto often contains cheese and pine nuts as well, but although traditional pistou contains neither, I like to add a small amount of toasted pine nuts to my pistou for extra flavor. I do omit the cheese, however, to avoid masking the vibrant flavors of the abundant summer vegetables in this soup. Topped with the bright green pistou, each bowl is a gorgeous testament to summer's rich bounty.

For a heartier dish, add 1 cup cooked small pasta, such as macaroni, just before serving, and heat the soup for about 2 minutes to warm it through.

SEE PHOTOGRAPH ON PAGE 58.

IF USING DRIED BEANS, rinse and pick over them, discarding any stones. Put the beans in a large bowl and cover them with a generous amount of cold water. Let stand overnight, then drain and rinse. Fresh beans do not need to be soaked.

Put the beans in a medium saucepan with the ½ onion, ½ carrot, ½ rib celery, thyme, and bay leaf, and add enough cold water to cover by 2 inches. Bring to a boil, skimming off any foam as it rises. Reduce the heat and simmer the beans until tender, about 30 minutes for fresh beans and 1½ hours for dry. Remove the pot from the heat and gently stir in 1 teaspoon salt. As the beans cool, they will absorb the seasoning from the water. Set aside to cool.

In a small, heavy skillet over medium heat, toast the pine nuts until they are lightly browned and fragrant, about 4 minutes. Remove the nuts from the skillet and set them aside to cool.

Finely chop the remaining onion, carrot, and celery and the leek. In a large, heavy-bottomed pot, heat 2 tablespoons of the olive oil over medium heat. Add the chopped onion and a pinch of salt and cook until the onion begins to soften, about 4 minutes. Add the chopped carrot, celery, and leek and cook until all the vegetables are soft, about 8 minutes. Add the diced tomato and cook until it begins to caramelize and the juice has reduced, 3 to 4 minutes. Add the summer squash and potato with a pinch of salt. Stir to coat with the oil and cook until heated through, about 1 minute.

Add the stock and bring to a boil. Reduce the heat and simmer until the potatoes begin to soften, 15 to 20 minutes. Add the green beans and cook until they are tender, about 5 minutes.

Remove and discard the vegetables and aromatics from the reserved beans. Add the beans and their cooking liquid to the soup. Bring back to a boil and adjust the seasoning with salt and pepper.

Meanwhile, with a mortar and pestle, pound the garlic clove to a paste with a pinch of salt. Add the toasted pine nuts and pound them with the garlic. Add the basil leaves and a small splash of olive oil and pound to a fine paste. Alternatively, finely chop the ingredients together. Slowly work in enough olive oil—up to ½ cup total—to loosen the pistou until it falls off a spoon easily; it should not be too thick. Season with salt and pepper.

Ladle the soup into warmed bowls and top each with a spoonful of pistou. Serve immediately.

gazpacho

8 ounces ripe red tomatoes (about
    1 large)

1 red bell pepper

1 serrano chile

1 large cucumber

1 red onion

Kosher salt and freshly ground
    black pepper

½ cup extra-virgin olive oil, plus
    more for serving

1 pint mixed cherry tomatoes, such
    as Sweet 100s, Sun Gold, or red
    pear, cut in half

¼ cup fresh flat-leaf parsley leaves,
    coarsely chopped

2 tablespoons chopped fresh chives

2 tablespoons red wine vinegar

**SERVES 4 AS A LIGHT MAIN COURSE
OR 6 AS AN APPETIZER**

We served this gazpacho at a dinner at Knoll Farm in Brentwood, California. The hot summers at Knoll Farm bring a great profusion of sweet, juicy tomatoes of every size and color. Use as many different kinds of cherry tomatoes as you can, as we did on that day, for their varied flavors and stunning colors help make this version of gazpacho more special than most.

DICE THE RED TOMATOES. Cut the bell pepper and the chile in half and remove the seeds and stems. Coarsely chop the pepper and chile. Be careful not to handle the hot chile seeds too much with your bare hands and to wash your hands, knife, and the cutting board thoroughly after chopping the chile. Peel the cucumber and remove the seeds. Roughly chop three-quarters of the cucumber. Cut the remaining piece into small dice for garnish and set aside. Peel the red onion and cut into small dice. Set half of it aside for garnish.

Working in batches, combine the chopped tomatoes, bell pepper, chile, cucumber, and onion in a blender and season with salt. Blend on low speed until the vegetables begin to turn into a purée. Turn off and scrape down the sides of the blender. Turn the speed to high and slowly pour in the olive oil. Blend until very smooth. Pour though a mesh strainer into a large bowl, using a wooden spoon to press the mixture against the sides of the strainer to extract all the liquid possible. There should be 2 to 3 tablespoons solids left behind in the strainer; reblend the mixture if you have more than that.

Stir the reserved diced cucumber and onion along with the cherry tomatoes, parsley, chives, and red wine vinegar into the blended soup. Season with salt and pepper to taste.

Refrigerate the soup for at least 8 hours or overnight. To serve, ladle into chilled soup bowls and drizzle with olive oil.

pumpkin and persimmon soup

SERVES 6 TO 8

Pumpkins and persimmons ripen at about the same time of year and the first glimpse of them at farmers' markets signifies to me that summer has begun to turn to fall. The Fuyu persimmons are best for this soup when they are extra ripe and slightly soft; their sweetness nicely complements pumpkin's earthy flavor.

1 medium Sugarpie, Cinderella, Baby Bear, or other pumpkin (about 4 pounds)

1 pound Fuyu persimmons

1 tablespoon extra-virgin olive oil

1 tablespoon unsalted butter

1 onion, chopped

1 fresh or dried bay leaf

Kosher salt

2 carrots, chopped

Freshly ground black pepper

2 quarts Chicken Stock or Vegetable Stock (pages 208 or 207) or low-sodium broth

½ cup heavy cream

1 tablespoon white wine vinegar

CUT THE ENDS off the pumpkin and place it on a flat surface. Using a serrated knife, gently saw down the length of the pumpkin to remove the peel. Cut the pumpkin in half and scoop out the seeds with a spoon. Cut the pumpkin into ½-inch pieces. Set aside.

Peel the persimmons and remove the tops. Cut into ½-inch pieces, removing any seeds. Set aside.

Heat the olive oil and butter in a Dutch oven or other large, heavy-bottomed pot over medium-low heat. When the foaming subsides, add the onion, bay leaf, and a pinch of salt. Cook, stirring frequently, until the onion is translucent, about 8 minutes. Add the carrots, and stir to combine. Cook until the carrots begin to soften, about 5 minutes. Add the pumpkin and salt and pepper to taste and stir to coat with the fat. Cook for 2 minutes.

Add the stock and raise the heat to medium-high. Bring to a boil, reduce the heat, and add the persimmons. Simmer until the vegetables are tender, about 20 minutes. Discard the bay leaf.

Working in batches, transfer the soup to a food processor or blender and blend until smooth. Return the soup to the pot and bring back to a boil. If the soup seems too thick, adjust the consistency with a little stock. Stir in the cream. Remove the pot from the heat and stir in the vinegar. Taste and adjust the seasoning with salt and pepper. Serve in warmed bowls.

Olive Oil

Olive oil's flavor depends on which of hundreds of varieties of olive is used and when they are harvested. When olives are still green, they give the oil peppery, spicy, and grassy characteristics. As the olives ripen, the oil made from them is mellower and fruitier. Riper olives also contain more oil, but many people feel the better-quality oils come from greener olives. Often the producer blends oils from different parts of the harvest to create a well-balanced oil. A large farm with many trees may produce several types of olive oil, including oil that comes purely from the first part of the harvest as well as a blend of oils pressed at different times during the season.

Olio nuovo, or new oil, is the term used for unfiltered olive oil bottled especially for selling during the first month or two after it has been processed. Olio nuovo has a very strong flavor, although if the bottle is kept for longer than two months the solids will settle and the flavor of the oil will mellow. To me, however, there is nothing more heavenly than freshly grilled slices of country bread rubbed with a clove of garlic, drizzled with olio nuovo, and sprinkled with sea salt. (Of course, this is also known as *bruschetta*, and there's another, somewhat more adorned version on page 28.) Olio nuovo is available only during the olive harvest, so keep your eyes open for it in the fall.

The term *extra-virgin* carries real meaning. California olive oil must meet specific guidelines to be labeled extra-virgin by the California Olive Oil Council: It must be cold-processed, meaning the olive paste must never exceed 27°C (80.6°F) during processing; no heat or chemical processes may be used to extract more oil; and the oil must contain no more than 0.5 percent oleic acids. Finally, the oil must also pass a blind-tasting panel that checks both for characteristic underlying flavors of extra-virgin oil, such as artichoke, apple, grass, black pepper, and melon, and for defects, such as a rancid or cooked flavor, winey characteristics, or the taste of mold. Often, if a defect is detected, the oil is sent to a factory where it is stripped completely of its flavor and a small amount of extra-virgin olive oil is added to make a product that is then sold as *pure olive oil* or simply *olive oil*. True extra-virgin olive oil comes from a single extraction. If any oil is extracted from the remaining solids, this is probably achieved by heat or chemical means, and the resulting oil is labeled *refined*.

I use extra-virgin olive oil for just about everything in cooking except deep-frying; olive oil burns at too low a temperature for that.

baby turnip soup

SERVES 4

1½ pounds baby turnips with
    greens
3 tablespoons extra-virgin olive oil,
    plus more for serving
2 onions, chopped
Kosher salt
3 ribs celery, chopped
1 carrot, chopped
2 fresh or dried bay leaves
3 sprigs fresh thyme
4 quarts Chicken Stock (page 208)
    or low-sodium broth, plus more if
    needed
Freshly ground black pepper

You can use any baby turnip for this soup, but the best is a variety called Tokyo that is growing in popularity. Keep your eye out for them in the early fall, for this is really a different soup when made with these turnips, which are sweeter and more delicate than other turnips. Use an olive oil with a bit of spiciness (see page 67) for garnish.

BRING A POT of salted water to a boil and prepare a bowl of ice water. While the water is heating, remove the greens from the turnips and set aside. Peel the turnips, chop them, and set aside. Remove any tough stems from the turnip greens. Cook the turnip greens in the boiling water just until tender, about 2 minutes. Drain them and plunge them immediately into the ice water to stop the cooking and keep their bright green color. When the greens are cool, remove them from the water and squeeze out any liquid. Chop the greens into ½-inch pieces. Set aside.

In a heavy-bottomed stockpot, heat 3 tablespoons olive oil over medium heat. Add the onions and a pinch of salt and cook until translucent, about 8 minutes. Add the turnips, celery, carrot, bay leaves, and thyme sprigs and season with salt. Cook, stirring occasionally, until the vegetables begin to soften, about 10 minutes.

Add the chicken stock, bring to a boil, and then reduce the heat. Simmer until the vegetables are very soft, about 1 hour.

Remove the pot from the heat and remove and discard the thyme sprigs and bay leaves. Purée the soup in batches in a food processor or blender until smooth. Taste and adjust the seasoning with salt and pepper. Put the soup back in the pot and bring back to a boil. Stir in the chopped turnip greens. Ladle into warmed bowls, drizzle with olive oil, and serve.

bread soup with beans and kale

SERVES 8 TO 10

At a dinner at Hidden Villa Farm in Los Altos, California, where the blue-black leaves of dinosaur kale stretched out in rows running alongside our table, we served this soup under the canopy of an aged chestnut tree. As is true for many hearty soups, the flavor of this one will improve by sitting for a day or two.

1 cup dried cannelini, cranberry, zolfini, or other beans or 2 cups shelled fresh beans (from about 2 pounds in the pod)

Kosher salt

Freshly ground black pepper

3 tablespoons extra-virgin olive oil, plus more for serving

2 onions, halved and thinly sliced

2 carrots, finely chopped

3 ribs celery, finely chopped

1 dried red chile, chopped, or ¼ teaspoon crushed red pepper flakes

1 sprig fresh rosemary

1 tablespoon tomato paste

8 ounces dinosaur kale, also called cavolo nero

4 quarts Chicken Stock (page 208) or low-sodium broth

1 loaf stale country bread

Freshly grated Parmesan or Pecorino cheese, for serving

IF USING DRIED BEANS, rinse and pick over them, discarding any stones. Place the beans in a large bowl and cover with cold water by 2 inches. Let stand overnight, then drain and rinse. (Fresh beans do not need to be soaked.)

Place the beans in a large pot and cover with cold water. Bring to a boil, skimming off any foam as it rises. Reduce the heat and simmer the beans until tender, about 30 minutes for fresh beans and 1½ hours for dried. Remove the pot from the heat and gently stir 1½ teaspoons salt and some black pepper into the cooking liquid. As the beans cool, they will absorb the seasoning from the water. Set aside to cool.

In a Dutch oven or other large, heavy-bottomed pot, heat the olive oil over low heat. Add the onions and a pinch of salt. Cook, stirring occasionally, until the onions are soft and translucent, about 10 minutes.

Add the carrots, celery, chile, and rosemary to the onions and season with salt and pepper. Cook, stirring occasionally, until all of the vegetables soften and become fragrant, about 10 minutes. Add the tomato paste and stir to coat the vegetables. Cook until the tomato paste begins to caramelize and become sweet, about 3 minutes.

In the meantime, wash the kale and strip off the stems, including the tough rib that runs up the leaves. Chop the kale into 1-inch pieces. Add it to the vegetables and season to taste. When the greens have wilted a bit, add enough of the chicken stock to cover. Raise the heat to medium-high and bring to a boil. Reduce the heat and simmer until the kale is tender, 15 to 20 minutes.

Strain the beans and add them to the pot along with the remaining stock. Simmer for 5 to 10 minutes. Season with salt and pepper to taste. Remove and discard the rosemary sprig.

Remove and discard the crust from the bread and tear the bread into 2-inch pieces. Add the bread to the soup a few pieces at a time, stirring after each addition so all of the bread is completely moistened. The soup should begin to thicken once the bread absorbs the liquid; when all of the bread is added, the soup will be very thick.

Ladle into warmed bowls, grate some cheese on top, and drizzle with extra-virgin olive oil. Serve.

Blossom chips

Pickled carrots/fennel

Tomato - stuffed

Bean salad

Tartare

eggplant

Olives

Sardines - grill

Zuchini

Baby Leeks

Beef

Sauce

Potatoes

chestnut soup with porcini relish

SERVES 4

Nothing says autumn to me like the smell of cooking porcini or the earthy taste of chestnuts. This recipe uses both to great effect, transforming the chestnuts into a creamy soup and the porcini into a tangy relish.

1 pound fresh porcini mushrooms or 2 ounces dried

1 pound fresh chestnuts in the shell or about 14.5 ounces canned or frozen peeled chestnuts

3 tablespoons extra-virgin olive oil

3 tablespoons unsalted butter

1 large onion, chopped

2 fresh or dried bay leaves

Kosher salt

3 celery ribs, chopped

About 6 cups Chicken Stock (page 208) or low-sodium broth

1 large shallot, minced

2 tablespoons sherry vinegar

Freshly ground black pepper

CLEAN FRESH porcini mushrooms with a damp cloth and coarsely chop them.

If using dried porcini, place them in a medium bowl and pour hot water over them to cover. Soak for 30 minutes, until the mushrooms are softened. Lift out the mushrooms with your hands, squeezing out the excess water from them. Coarsely chop the mushrooms and set aside. Pour the soaking liquid into a bowl, leaving behind the sediment at the bottom of the bowl. Set aside.

Meanwhile, if using fresh chestnuts, use a sharp knife to cut an X in the rounded side. Bring a pot of water to a boil and add the chestnuts. Return the water to a boil and boil the chestnuts for about 10 minutes to loosen the shells and inner skins. Remove the chestnuts with a slotted spoon. Peel off the shells and remove the brown skins. Some skins will be easier to remove than others; return any chestnuts with particularly stubborn skins to the boiling water for another minute. Do not worry about keeping the chestnuts intact. Place all the flesh in a bowl and set aside.

In a large, heavy-bottomed saucepan, melt 2 tablespoons of the olive oil and 2 tablespoons of the butter over medium-low heat. When the foaming subsides, add the onion and bay leaves with a pinch of salt. Cook, stirring occasionally, until the onion is translucent, about 8 minutes. Add the celery and continue cooking until golden, another 10 minutes. Add the chestnuts, season with salt, and stir to coat with the fat. Add enough chicken stock to cover and bring to a boil. Lower the heat and simmer gently until the chestnuts are very soft, 25 to 30 minutes, adding more chicken stock as needed to keep the chestnuts just covered. Remove and discard the bay leaves.

While the chestnuts are cooking, in a medium saucepan, heat the remaining 1 tablespoon olive oil and 1 tablespoon butter over low heat. Add the shallot, and cook, stirring occasionally, until soft and golden, about 10 minutes. Add the porcini to the pan with a pinch of salt and stir to combine. Raise the heat to medium-low and cook about 20 minutes, adding chicken stock or the porcini soaking liquid about ¼ cup at a time as needed when the pan is dry. When the mushrooms are very soft and the pan is dry, remove the pan from the heat and stir in the vinegar. Season with salt and pepper.

Working in batches, transfer the soup to a food processor or blender and process until smooth. Return the soup to the pot and thin with more stock if necessary. Adjust the seasoning with salt and pepper. Serve the soup in warmed bowls with a spoonful of the porcini relish on top.

farro soup
with greens

SERVES 4 TO 6

Related to spelt or emmer wheat, farro has a fantastic nutty taste and chewy texture, which in this soup
play very well against the sharp, slightly bitter flavor of
hearty greens. This dish can make great use of whatever greens are in your garden. Farro can be found at
Italian and specialty markets. Look for *semiperlato,* or
semi-pearled, farro, which has had some of the hard
hull removed. It is hard to overcook farro, but don't
look for it to soften as much as barley or other grains.

1 cup semipearled farro

Kosher salt

2 tablespoons extra-virgin olive oil,
   plus more for serving

1 large onion, cut into small dice

1 carrot, peeled and cut into
   small dice

1 leek, white and light green parts
   only, cut into small dice

1 clove garlic, minced

1 small dried chile, finely chopped,
   or ¼ teaspoon crushed red
   pepper flakes

1 tablespoon tomato paste

1 bunch of kale, chard, mustard
   greens, or cabbage, coarsely
   chopped

About 6 cups Chicken Stock
   (page 208) or low-sodium broth

Freshly ground black pepper

Freshly grated Parmesan or
   Pecorino cheese, for serving
   (optional)

PLACE THE FARRO in a pot, cover it with cold
water, and add 1 teaspoon salt. Bring the water
to a boil, reduce the heat, and simmer until the
farro is just tender, about 20 minutes. Remove
the pot from the heat.

In the meantime, heat the olive oil in a
Dutch oven or other large, heavy-bottomed pot
with a tight-fitting lid over medium heat. Add the
onion and a pinch of salt and cook, stirring
occasionally, until the onion is soft, about
8 minutes. Add the carrot and leek and another
pinch of salt and continue cooking until the
vegetables begin to soften, another 10 minutes.

Move some of the vegetables to one side of the pot and add the garlic and chile to the
open space. Cook until fragrant, about 30 seconds. Mix the garlic into the vegetables and
add the tomato paste. Cook until the tomato paste begins to caramelize and become
sweet, about 5 minutes. Add the greens, season with salt, and stir to combine. Cook until
the greens wilt and release some of their liquid, about 5 minutes. Add about 2 cups of the
stock and bring to a simmer.

Add the farro and its cooking liquid along with enough of the remaining stock to cover the ingredients. Simmer for 20 minutes, adding more stock if necessary to keep the ingredients covered with liquid. When all of the vegetables are tender and the flavors have combined, adjust the seasoning with salt and pepper and cover the pot. Let stand for 10 minutes.

Ladle the soup into warmed bowls and drizzle with extra-virgin olive oil. Offer the cheese for grating on top if desired.

vegetables

GRILLED ASPARAGUS WITH KUMQUAT VINAIGRETTE

———

POTATOES COOKED IN THE COALS

———

BAKED FRESH SHELL BEANS WITH ROSEMARY

———

FRIED ARTICHOKES

———

STEWED GREEN BEANS

———

MARINATED ROASTED BEETS

———

BEET GREENS WITH LEMON JUICE AND EXTRA-VIRGIN OLIVE OIL

———

DEEP-FRIED OKRA WITH A BUTTERMILK-SEMOLINA CRUST

———

RAINBOW CHARD TART

———

CELERY GRATIN

———

GREEN GARLIC AND POTATO GRATIN

grilled asparagus with kumquat vinaigrette

SERVES 4

As soon as the first asparagus appears in springtime markets, grab it along with a container of the last kumquats of the season. The combination—smoky, herbal asparagus against sweet, tangy kumquats—is exquisite and, in general, possible for just a few weeks.

1 lemon

1 small shallot, minced

1 pound fresh asparagus

¼ cup plus 1 tablespoon extra-virgin olive oil, plus more if needed

Kosher salt and freshly ground black pepper

10 kumquats

PREPARE a medium-hot grill; the coals should be ashed over, with no visible flame.

Remove the zest from the lemon with a vegetable peeler and chop it finely. Squeeze the juice from the lemon and combine it in a small bowl with the zest and shallot. Set aside to macerate for about 10 minutes.

Snap the fibrous ends off the asparagus and discard. Toss the asparagus with 1 tablespoon olive oil and season with salt and pepper. Set aside.

Add a pinch of salt to the lemon juice mixture and, whisking constantly, slowly pour in the ¼ cup olive oil. Taste for acidity and add more oil if the dressing is too tart. Thinly slice the kumquats crosswise, removing any seeds as you go. Mix them into the vinaigrette and season with salt and pepper.

When the grill is ready, grill the asparagus, turning once, until it is tender and nicely marked, about 5 minutes total.

Arrange the asparagus on a platter and pour the kumquat vinaigrette on top. Serve hot or at room temperature.

potatoes cooked in the coals

2 pounds small potatoes, such as
    Red Bliss, fingerling, Ruby
    Crescent, or Yellow Finn
Extra-virgin olive oil
Kosher salt
6 cloves garlic, crushed
4 fresh or dried bay leaves
8 sprigs fresh thyme

This is a great way to cook your potatoes while grilling the rest of the meal. They take on a wonderful smoky flavor. Don't skimp on the heavy-duty foil, however—and make sure the package does specifically state "heavy-duty"—or the potatoes will be charred instead of pleasantly smoky.

SCRUB THE POTATOES and dry them on a towel. In a large bowl, toss the potatoes with a drizzle of olive oil and season generously with salt.

Prepare 6 large squares of heavy-duty aluminum foil. Distribute the potatoes between 2 of the squares and divide between them the garlic, bay leaves, and thyme sprigs. Fold over the foil and crimp the edges to seal. Wrap each package in another square of aluminum foil, folding and crimping the edges to seal. Finally, wrap each in the last square of foil, folding and crimping the edges to seal.

Place the packages directly in coals that are completely ashed over; there should be no visible flame. Cook, using tongs to turn the packages over and shake them slightly from time to time, until the potatoes are tender, about 30 minutes.

Remove the potatoes from their packages and spoon onto a warmed platter or into a serving bowl.

baked fresh shell beans with rosemary

4 cups shelled fresh beans, such as cranberry, flageolet, or cannellini (from about 4 pounds in the pod), or 2 cups dried beans

1 small onion, halved

1 small carrot, halved

1 rib celery, cut in 3 pieces

2 sprigs rosemary

Kosher salt and freshly ground black pepper

4 tablespoons olive oil

2 cloves garlic

3 ripe tomatoes, coarsely chopped, or 1 (14.5-ounce) can chopped tomatoes

¼ cup red wine

1½ cups coarse fresh bread crumbs (from about 3 cups cubed crustless bread)

This recipe can be made any time of the year just by changing the main ingredients to fit the season. During the summer, when abundant fresh shell beans and ripe tomatoes are prepared in this simple way, the dish is special enough to be served on its own or as a stunning side dish alongside grilled pork or chicken. During the winter, dried beans and canned tomatoes make a hearty side dish, delicious with roasted meat or poultry.

IF USING DRIED BEANS, rinse and pick over them, discarding any stones. Place the beans in a large bowl and cover with cold water by 2 inches. Let stand overnight, then drain and rinse.

In a large pot, combine the beans, onion, carrot, celery, and 1 sprig of the rosemary. Cover with cold water and bring to a boil, skimming off any foam as it rises. Reduce the heat and simmer the beans until tender, about 30 minutes for fresh beans and 1½ hours for dry. Remove the pot from the heat and gently stir in 1½ teaspoons salt and some pepper. As the beans cool, they will absorb the seasoning from the water.

In a large skillet with steep sides, heat 1 tablespoon of the olive oil over medium heat. Add the garlic and the remaining rosemary sprig and cook briefly until fragrant but not browned. Add the tomatoes with a pinch each of salt and pepper. Simmer over low heat until the sauce begins to dry out and become sweet, about 20 minutes. Stir in the red wine and cook for an additional 5 to 10 minutes, until the wine has evaporated and the sauce has a sweet, concentrated flavor. Remove the rosemary sprig and discard.

Heat the oven to 375°F.

Strain the beans, reserving 1 cup of the cooking liquid. Remove and discard the vegetables and the rosemary sprig. Add the beans to the tomato sauce along with the reserved 1 cup bean liquid. Stir to combine and cook together over medium-low heat for 5 minutes to allow the flavors to blend. Season with salt and pepper.

In a small bowl, combine the bread crumbs with the remaining 3 tablespoons olive oil. Stir to coat the crumbs well with oil.

Pour the beans into a 2-quart baking dish with 2-inch sides. Sprinkle the bread crumbs over the beans to completely cover the surface. Bake the beans for 30 to 40 minutes, until the top is bubbly and golden. Remove from the oven and let cool for 10 minutes before serving.

fried artichokes

4 lemons

6 small artichokes

Vegetable oil, for deep-frying

¾ cup unbleached all-purpose flour

Kosher salt

2 large eggs

1½ cups fresh bread crumbs
(from about 3 cups cubed
crustless bread)

**SERVES 6 TO 8 AS AN APPETIZER;
OR 4 TO 6 AS A SIDE DISH**

Although Castroville, the self-proclaimed "Artichoke Capital of the World," is just down the road from my home in California, some of the best artichokes I've ever had were in Matanuska Valley, Alaska. At our dinner there we prepared farm-fresh chokes at a dinner served at the base of breathtaking Pioneer Peak. Traditionally served as an appetizer, fried artichokes are also nice served as a side dish with fish or meat dishes.

FILL A LARGE BOWL with cold water. Cut 2 of the lemons in half and juice them into the water; toss in the lemon rinds as well. Remove the tough outer leaves from the artichokes so only the tender, light yellow ones are showing. Trim about 1 inch from the tops. Trim the bottoms, leaving some stem attached and using a paring knife to peel off the green layer from the stem. Put the cleaned artichokes in the acidulated water. When all of the artichokes have been cleaned, cut them in half and use a spoon or paring knife to scoop out the choke and the pale pink, very immature leaves. Cut each half in thirds so you have small wedges and return them to the acidulated water until all are prepared.

Cut the remaining 2 lemons into wedges for serving and set aside.

Pour the oil into a large, deep pot, such as a Dutch oven, so it is at least 2½ inches deep but comes no more than halfway up the sides of the pot. Attach a candy or deep-frying thermometer to the side of the pot and heat the oil over medium heat to 375°F.

While the oil is heating, put the flour in a shallow dish and season with salt. In another shallow dish, beat the eggs. Put the bread crumbs in a separate dish. Remove the artichokes from the water and drain well on a towel. Dredge the artichokes in the flour, then dip them in the egg, and then coat them lightly in the bread crumbs.

Using a mesh skimmer to move the artichokes in and out of the hot oil, fry the artichokes in batches until golden brown, 45 seconds to 1 minute. Drain on paper towels and sprinkle with salt. Serve warm with the lemon wedges.

stewed green beans

SERVES 4

1 pound green beans, such as Blue
   Lake, runner, Romano, or
   Kentucky Wonder

1 small onion

2 tablespoons extra-virgin olive oil,
   plus more for serving

3 anchovy fillets, coarsely chopped

1 clove garlic, minced

1 small dried chile pepper,
   chopped, or ¼ teaspoon crushed
   red pepper flakes

Kosher salt

4 medium ripe tomatoes, chopped,
   or (14.5-ounce) can chopped
   tomatoes

Freshly ground black pepper to
   taste

This recipe really concentrates the flavor and brings out the sweetness of the beans and the tomatoes. It is a delicious accompaniment to grilled and roasted meats or barbecued chicken.

SEE PHOTOGRAPH ON PAGE 165.

REMOVE THE TOPS from the beans and cut any larger ones in half. Cut the onion in half lengthwise. Trim off the top and bottom of each half and thinly slice lengthwise.

In a heavy-bottomed pot over medium-low heat, heat 1 tablespoon of the olive oil until hot but not smoking. Add the onion and cook, stirring frequently, until soft and golden, about 10 minutes. Move the onion to the side of the pan and add the remaining tablespoon olive oil to the center of the pan. Add the anchovies, garlic, and chile and cook, stirring occasionally, until fragrant and the anchovy has begun to break down, about 1 minute. Stir the onions into the anchovy mixture.

Add the beans and a pinch of salt and stir to combine. Cook for another 2 minutes. Add the tomatoes with a pinch of salt and simmer gently for about 10 minutes or until the beans are tender and the tomato juices have reduced and sweetened. Add a bit of water if the pan becomes too dry. Season with salt and pepper to taste.

Serve drizzled with extra-virgin olive oil.

marinated
roasted beets

Roasting beets is a great way to concentrate their sugars and bring out amazing earthy flavors. Marinated in this way, they are wonderfully versatile. Serve simply on a green salad or mixed with crisp spring vegetables. They are also fantastic paired with Pickled Trout (page 132). Choose small- to medium-sized beets—about 5 or 6 small ones to a pound—as the large ones tend to be woody. If you use a colorful mix of beets, cook and marinate them separately so their colors don't run together. Use the beet greens in Beet Greens with Lemon Juice and Extra-Virgin Olive Oil (page 88).

1 pound red, Chioggia, or gold beets, tops removed

1 tablespoon vegetable oil

Kosher salt

3 sprigs thyme or 1 sprig rosemary

1 small shallot, minced

3 tablespoons red wine vinegar

$\frac{1}{3}$ cup extra-virgin olive oil

Freshly ground black pepper

HEAT THE OVEN to 375°F.

Scrub the beets and pat them dry. Place them in a small baking dish, toss them with the vegetable oil, and season with salt. Add the thyme sprigs to the pan along with about $\frac{1}{3}$ cup water. Cover the pan tightly with aluminum foil. Roast in the oven until the beets can be easily pierced with a knife, about 45 minutes for medium beets; cooking time will vary depending on the size of the beets. Remove the foil and allow the beets to sit at room temperature just until cool enough to handle.

To make the marinade, in a small bowl combine the shallot and vinegar and set aside to macerate for 10 minutes. Add a pinch of salt and slowly whisk in the olive oil until well combined.

Using your hands, peel the beets (you may wish to wear rubber gloves if handling red beets, as the juices will stain your hands). Cut the beets into $\frac{1}{8}$-inch rounds or $\frac{1}{4}$-inch wedges and place them in a medium bowl.

Pour the marinade over the beets and stir gently with a wooden spoon to thoroughly coat the beets with the marinade. Season to taste with salt and pepper. Let sit at room temperature for 30 minutes before serving.

beet greens with lemon juice and extra-virgin olive oil

1 bunch beet greens (10 to 12 ounces)
4 tablespoons extra-virgin olive oil
Kosher salt
1 clove garlic, minced
1 tablespoon fresh lemon juice
Freshly ground black pepper

Beets greens are the gift you get with almost every bunch of fresh beets you buy, but how often do they end up in the compost heap (or, worse, garbage) instead of on your plate? I'm perplexed by this waste, considering how delicious and healthy beet greens are, but it's not entirely surprising: In these busy times, who has time to deal with the trimmings? Here is a recipe I hope will make you think of beet greens as something much more than the leaves attached to your favorite vegetable. Glistening green leaves and magenta stems, simply prepared, are reminiscent of the flavor and aroma of the beet itself. Try to buy beets with greens that are still crisp and not wilted or yellowed. Beet greens can also be used in place of spinach, kale, or chard in any recipe for cooked greens.

WASH THE BEET GREENS. Remove the stems and chop them into a small dice. Coarsely chop the leaves and set them aside.

Heat 1 tablespoon of the olive oil in a heavy-bottomed skillet over medium-low heat. Add the chopped beet stems and a pinch of salt. Cook, stirring occasionally, until the stems are nearly tender, about 8 minutes. Push the beet stems to one side of the pan and add the garlic to the other side. Cook until fragrant but not brown, about 1 minute. Stir the garlic into the stems. Add the chopped beet leaves and season with salt. Stir in a splash of water and cook until the leaves are tender, 8 to 10 minutes.

In a small bowl, whisk together the lemon juice and remaining 3 tablespoons olive oil with a pinch of salt.

Remove the pan from the heat, pour the dressing on top, and stir to combine. Season with salt and pepper. Serve hot.

deep-fried okra with a buttermilk-semolina crust

Vegetable oil, for deep-frying
1 pound young okra pods
1½ cups buttermilk
1½ cups semolina flour
1 cup unbleached all-purpose flour
Kosher salt
Lemon-caper mayonnaise (page
    206) or lemon slices, for serving

At Full Moon Farm in Athens, Georgia, the row of flowering okra was taller than the bus. Not only did the row give us more than enough okra for the feast, it also gave us a welcome bit of evening shade.

It is important to fry only a few okra pods at a time; if the pot is overcrowded, the temperature of the oil will drop and the okra will become soggy instead of crisp. Serve these as a side to fish or poultry dishes, or pile them high on a platter with bowls of mayonnaise for dipping and serve as an appetizer.

POUR THE OIL into a large, deep pot, such as a Dutch oven, so it is at least 2½ inches deep but comes no more than halfway up the sides of the pot. Attach a candy or deep-frying thermometer to the side of the pot and heat the oil to 375°F over medium heat.

While the oil is heating, remove the stems of the okra, being careful not to cut open the pods. Pour the buttermilk into a medium bowl. Mix together the semolina, flour, and a pinch of salt in a wide, shallow baking dish or pan. Line a baking sheet with parchment paper.

Dip an okra pod in the buttermilk, shake off the excess, and then place it in the semolina mixture, coating on all sides. Tap off any excess and put the okra on the parchment-lined sheet pan. Repeat with the remaining okra.

When the oil is ready, use a mesh skimmer to move the okra in and out of the hot oil. Fry the okra in batches until golden brown, 2 to 3 minutes. Remove the okra pods from the oil and transfer them to paper towels to drain.

When all of the okra has been fried, season with salt and serve warm with lemon-caper mayonnaise or lemon slices, or on their own.

rainbow chard tart

1¾ cups unbleached all-purpose
   flour
Kosher salt
5 tablespoons unsalted butter,
   at room temperature
¼ cup plus 2 tablespoons
   extra-virgin olive oil
1 to 3 tablespoons ice water
1 large bunch rainbow chard
   (about ¾ pound)
1 sprig fresh rosemary
1 large egg yolk
1 onion, finely diced
1 clove garlic, minced
3 large eggs
⅓ cup heavy cream
¾ cup freshly grated Parmesan
   or Pecorino cheese (about
   2½ ounces)
Freshly ground black pepper

SERVES 6 TO 8

With its stems of vibrant red, orange, yellow, pink, and palest green, plus its deep green leaves, rainbow chard is one of the most beautiful leafy greens on earth. The abundance of fresh chard and the olive oil in the crust give this rustic tart an earthy, nutty flavor. And with just enough custard to hold the filling together, those flavors are really the stars here. The pat-in-pan crust makes it easy to put together.

SEE PHOTOGRAPH ON PAGE 78.

COMBINE THE FLOUR and ½ teaspoon salt in the bowl of a food processor and pulse a few times to mix them. Add the butter and pulse until the mixture resembles coarse bread crumbs. Pour in ¼ cup olive oil and pulse a few more times. Add the ice water a little at a time and pulse just until the dough begins to come together. Use your fingers to press it into the base and up the sides of a 10-inch tart pan with a removable base. Wrap loosely in plastic wrap and refrigerate for at least 1 hour.

Clean the chard leaves and remove the stems, reserving them. Trim the ends off the chard stems and discard. Cut the stems into small dice, about the same size as the onion. Cut the chard leaves in half lengthwise and then into 1-inch-wide strips. Strip the rosemary leaves from their stem and coarsely chop them.

Heat the oven to 400°F.

Remove the crust from the refrigerator. Bake until the crust is golden brown, 12 to 15 minutes. While the crust is baking, mix the egg yolk with a pinch of salt. Remove the crust from the oven and brush it with the egg yolk. Bake until the glaze is set, about 2 minutes. Remove the crust from the oven and set it aside.

Reduce the oven temperature to 375°F.

While the crust is baking, heat the remaining 2 tablespoons olive oil in a heavy-bottomed deep skillet over medium-low heat. Add the onion and a pinch of salt and cook, stirring occasionally, until the onion is soft and translucent, about 8 minutes. Add the chard stems and chopped rosemary. Cook, stirring occasionally, for 7 to 10 minutes, until the stems are tender. Clear a small space in the pan and add the garlic. Cook until fragrant, about 30 seconds, and then stir the garlic into the onion and chard stems. Raise the heat to medium. Stir in the chard leaves and season with salt. Cook until the leaves are wilted and soft and any liquid has evaporated, 7 to 10 minutes. Remove the pan from the heat and let cool.

Beat together the eggs and cream and season with salt and pepper. Add the chard mixture and then the grated cheese and mix well. Scrape the filling into the prepared shell.

Bake for 35 to 40 minutes, until just set. Let cool for at least 15 minutes before serving. Serve warm or at room temperature.

celery gratin

SERVES 4

1 bunch fresh celery, base trimmed

1 cup heavy cream

½ cup Chicken Stock or Vegetable Stock (pages 208 or 207) or low-sodium broth

2 cloves garlic, crushed

1 handful lovage leaves or 4 fresh thyme or summer savory sprigs

Kosher salt and freshly ground black pepper

1 cup fresh bread crumbs (from about 2 cups cubed crustless bread)

2 tablespoons extra-virgin olive oil

1 tablespoon unsalted butter, at room temperature

Here is a warming winter side dish that inspires new appreciation for celery, an often overlooked ingredient. It goes well with roasted beef, lamb, or game birds.

HEAT THE OVEN to 375°F. Butter the base and sides of a 1½-quart baking dish.

Wash the celery ribs. Remove the leaves and set them aside. Use a paring knife to strip any tough strings from the outer stalks. Cut the ribs into 2-inch-long pieces.

Bring a pot of salted water to a boil; prepare a bowl of ice water. Add the celery to the boiling water and cook until just tender, about 5 minutes. Drain the celery and plunge it into the ice water. Drain well.

Combine the cream, stock, garlic, and half of the lovage in a saucepan. Gently heat the mixture until it just starts to bubble. Remove the pan from the heat and cover. Let stand and infuse for about 5 minutes. Remove and discard the garlic and lovage.

Finely chop the reserved celery leaves and the remaining lovage. Line the base of the dish with half of the celery ribs, overlapping the pieces so the base is completely covered. Sprinkle half of the chopped celery leaves and half of the remaining lovage on top and season with salt and pepper. Ladle a bit of the cream mixture over the celery in the dish to moisten. Repeat with the remaining celery and chopped leaves and lovage. Pour in enough of the cream to come halfway up the sides of the dish. Dot the top with pieces of softened butter. Cover the dish with aluminum foil and bake in the oven for 30 minutes.

Remove from the oven; remove the foil; and increase the oven temperature to 425°F.

In a small bowl, combine the bread crumbs with the olive oil and stir well to thoroughly moisten the crumbs. Spread the bread crumbs over the celery. Return the dish to the oven uncovered. Cook until golden brown and bubbling, about 10 minutes.

Cool the gratin for 10 minutes before serving.

Claravale Dairy, Watsonville, California

Ron Garthwaite, of Claravale Dairy, has brought his heavenly milk, cream, and butter to many of our dinners. Claravale is a small raw milk dairy set just 100 yards from a cliff overlooking the coast in Santa Cruz County. I like to think it is the stunning setting that makes the cow's milk taste so good, but I think it actually has more to do with a few other factors. First, the size of the dairy: Ron has fewer than fifty cows, which keeps the operation manageable and makes it feasible to carefully monitor the well-being—and know the name—of every cow. Second, the cows are Jerseys, whose milk is higher in butterfat than that of the Holsteins preferred by most large-scale conventional dairies. Higher-butterfat milk is better for drinking and better by far for making cheese. Last, Claravale is a raw milk dairy, which means the milk is not pasteurized, or brought to a temperature high enough to kill any microorganisms that might be harmful; in short, it is not cooked. The thing about pasteurization, though, is that in addition to killing bad microorganisms, it also kills all sorts of microorganisms that might be beneficial. And it isn't necessary if your milk is clean to begin with.

Since the rise of mass food production, made possible in large part by the rise of pasteurization, raw milk has been looked upon skeptically by many, but I believe this suspicion is misplaced. The reality is that raw milk dairies are by and large exquisitely clean; they have to be not only because they are actually more rigorously monitored by state authorities than conventional dairies but also because they can't simply kill by cooking any dangerous microorganisms that may creep in if the conditions are less sanitary. But for me, the final test is in the taste: Raw milk has none of the cooked taste of pasteurized milk. You've probably been drinking pasteurized milk so long—likely your whole life—that you may not even realize it tastes cooked. But you don't have to take my word for it; you can check it out for yourself. Use Local Harvest (page 246) to find a source of raw milk near you and taste it next to your regular milk.

green garlic and potato gratin

SERVES 4 TO 6

3 to 4 stalks green garlic

2 cups heavy cream

6 sprigs fresh thyme

3 pounds waxy potatoes, peeled

Kosher salt and ground black
  pepper

One sure sign that spring has arrived is the appearance of long stalks of bright green garlic on farms and in farmers' markets. Green garlic is immature garlic. It looks a lot like a green onion but tastes of mild garlic. It can be used copiously if cooked or judiciously if raw wherever you would use garlic. For this recipe, if your stalks of green garlic are about the size of large scallions, four should be perfect. If they are bigger, three will be good.

CUT THE DARK GREEN ends off the green garlic and rinse them; reserve the pale stalks. Put the dark green ends in a small saucepan along with the cream and thyme. Heat the mixture over medium-low heat just to a boil. Remove from the heat, cover the pan, and let infuse for about 10 minutes.

Heat the oven to 400°F. Butter a 13 x 9-inch oval or other 2-quart baking dish.

Slice the reserved green garlic stalks in half lengthwise. Rinse them well under running water and then slice them thinly on a slant. Using a mandoline or sharp knife, slice the potatoes about ⅛ inch thick.

Arrange a layer of potato slices along the bottom of the dish, overlapping slightly so the bottom is completely covered. Season with salt and pepper and then ladle a bit of the cream over and sprinkle with some of the sliced green garlic. Repeat these layers, finishing with a layer of potatoes. Press down on the potatoes with your hands to flatten and then pour in the remaining cream. Cover the top with aluminum foil.

Bake for 1 hour. Remove the foil and increase the oven temperature to 450°F.

Return the dish to the oven and bake until the top is well browned and bubbly, 10 to 15 minutes. Remove from the oven and let stand for 15 minutes before serving.

grains and pasta

WILD RICE BAKED WITH CHICKEN, FENNEL, AND PORCINI

———

ENGLISH PEA AND FRESH MINT RISOTTO

———

JERUSALEM ARTICHOKE RISOTTO WITH FRESH BAY LEAVES

———

FARRO RISOTTO WITH BROCCOLI RABE

———

GOAT'S-MILK RICOTTA AND SPINACH GNOCCHI

———

PASTA WITH WALNUT SAUCE

———

NETTLE TAGLIATELLE WITH NETTLE PURÉE

———

SMOKY STURGEON AND POTATO RAVIOLI

wild rice baked with chicken, fennel, and porcini

SERVES 4 TO 6

This one-pot main dish can be made using fresh, meaty porcini mushrooms when they are ripe in the fall. When fennel's season extends beyond the porcini, into the winter and spring, dried porcini make an excellent substitute for fresh.

1 pound fresh or 2 ounces dried
   porcini mushrooms
1½ to 2½ cups Chicken Stock
   (page 208) or low-sodium broth
4 to 6 whole chicken thighs, with
   skin and bones (1½ to 2 pounds)
Kosher salt and ground black
   pepper
1 tablespoon extra-virgin olive oil
1 small onion, diced
2 medium fennel bulbs, diced
1 teaspoon fresh thyme leaves
1 cup wild rice

IF USING fresh mushrooms, clean them with a damp cloth. Halve or quarter any very large mushrooms, and then cut all the mushrooms into ¼-inch thick slices. Set aside.

If using dried porcini, place them in a medium bowl and add just enough hot water to cover. Let stand for 30 minutes, until the mushrooms are softened. Lift the mushrooms out with your fingers, squeezing the excess water back into the bowl. Chop the mushrooms coarsely and set them aside. Pour the soaking liquid into a measuring cup, leaving behind the sediment at the bottom of the bowl. Add enough chicken stock to make 2½ cups. Set aside.

Arrange one rack in the center of the oven and one 6 inches from the top. Heat the oven to 375°F.

Pat the chicken thighs dry with paper towels and season them with salt and pepper. Heat the olive oil in a large, ovenproof, straight-sided skillet with a tight-fitting lid over medium heat until hot but not smoking. Lay the chicken thighs in the pan, skin side down. Cook until nicely browned and then turn and brown the other side, 4 to 5 minutes per side. Transfer the chicken to a plate. Pour off all but 2 tablespoons of the fat from the pan.

Add the onion to the pan along with a pinch of salt. Reduce the heat to medium-low and cook the onion until it begins to sweat, about 4 minutes. Add the fennel and another pinch of salt. Cook until softened, stirring occasionally, about 5 minutes. Add the reserved porcini and the thyme leaves and season with salt. Cook until the mushrooms are tender and their liquid has evaporated, about 5 minutes for fresh porcini and about 2 minutes for dried.

Add the wild rice and stir to coat with the vegetables and oil. Pour in the 2½ cups stock. Tuck the chicken thighs, skin side up, into the vegetables. Bring the mixture to the boil on the stovetop and then cover with a tight-fitting lid. Place in the oven and cook until the rice grains are tender and have splayed open and the liquid is absorbed, 1 hour to 1¼ hours. Try not to check the rice before 1 hour; opening the lid releases all the vital steam from the pan.

Remove the pan from the oven and turn on the broiler.

Uncover the the pan and return to the oven, placing it on the top rack. Broil until the chicken skin is crisp, about 3 minutes. Remove from the oven and let rest for 5 minutes. Spoon onto warmed plates and serve.

english pea and fresh mint risotto

SERVES 6

Here two classic pairings—mint with peas and peas with rice—are combined in one dish for a brilliant marriage of bright herbal flavor and creamy texture. I make a light pea-vegetable stock from the pods to boost the pea flavor of the risotto.

2 pounds sweet English peas in the pod

2 small onions

1 carrot, coarsely chopped

1 rib celery, coarsely chopped

1 fresh or dried bay leaf

6 fresh mint sprigs

1 tablespoon extra-virgin olive oil, plus more for serving

3 tablespoons unsalted butter

Kosher salt

2 cups Carnaroli or Arborio rice

½ cup freshly grated Parmesan cheese (about 1½ ounces), plus more for serving

Freshly ground black pepper

SHELL THE PEAS (you should have 2 cups, more or less). Place the pods in a large pot. Peel and cut 1 of the onions in quarters and add it to the pot along with the carrot, celery, and bay leaf. Cover with cold water and bring to a boil. Reduce the heat and simmer until the stock has a nice pea flavor, 30 to 45 minutes. Strain the stock, discarding the solids, then return the stock to the pot and place over low heat to keep warm.

Bring a small pot of salted water to a boil and prepare a bowl of ice water. Cook ½ cup of the peas in the boiling salted water until tender, 2 to 6 minutes, depending on the age of the peas. Drain the peas and transfer to the ice water to stop the cooking. Drain well. Process the cooked peas in a blender until smooth, adding a little of the pea stock if necessary to help them along. Set aside.

Strip the mint leaves off 4 of the sprigs and coarsely chop them. Set aside.

Heat the olive oil and 1 tablespoon of the butter in a large, shallow pot over medium-low heat. Finely chop the remaining onion. When the foaming in the pan subsides, add the onion, remaining 2 sprigs mint, and a pinch of salt. Cook over low heat, stirring occasionally, until very soft, about 13 minutes. Add the rice and another pinch of salt and stir to coat with the oil. Raise the heat to medium and cook, stirring, until the rice is lightly toasted, about 2 minutes.

Add 1 ladleful of the hot pea stock, stirring constantly over medium to medium-high heat; the mixture should be bubbling. When the rice absorbs the stock and the mixture begins to look dry, add another ladleful, continuing to stir. Cook, stirring constantly and adding 1 ladleful of stock whenever the rice has absorbed the stock, until the rice is cooked about halfway, about 10 minutes. Add the remaining peas and continue to cook, adding stock and stirring constantly until the rice is creamy and the grains are al dente— soft on the outside with a slight bite in the center, about 10 minutes. The peas should be tender and still bright green. You may not need to use all of the pea stock; whatever is left over can be frozen.

Remove the mint sprigs and stir in the pea purée and the chopped fresh mint leaves. Remove from the heat and vigorously stir in the remaining 2 tablespoons butter and the grated Parmesan. Season with salt and pepper. Divide among 6 warmed plates and serve immediately. Offer more Parmesan cheese and extra-virgin olive oil to drizzle over the top, if desired.

jerusalem artichoke risotto with fresh bay leaves

At our dinner at Coleman Farm in Carpinteria, California, our table was set among towering Jerusalem artichoke plants growing up to twelve feet tall and topped with lovely yellow flowers. In this dish, nutty Jerusalem artichokes and aromatic fresh bay leaves combine to make an herbal, earthy risotto that smells heavenly. If you can choose only a few fresh herbs to grow in your container or backyard garden, I urge you to consider making bay one of them. Nothing compares to the fragrance and flavor of fresh bay, and the plant is a beautiful addition to any garden.

Juice of ½ lemon

8 ounces Jerusalem artichokes

2 quarts Chicken Stock (page 208) or low-sodium broth

2 tablespoons extra-virgin olive oil, plus more for serving

½ onion, finely diced

Kosher salt

2 bay leaves, preferably fresh

2 cups Carnaroli or Arborio rice

1 tablespoon unsalted butter

⅓ cup freshly grated Parmesan cheese (about 1¼ ounces), plus more for serving

Freshly ground black pepper

FILL A LARGE BOWL with water and add the lemon juice. Peel the Jerusalem artichokes and cut them into ¼-inch dice. Put them into the acidulated water to prevent them from discoloring. Set aside.

Bring the chicken stock to a simmer and then keep warm over low heat.

Heat the olive oil in a large, shallow, straight-sided pot over medium heat. Add the onion with a pinch of salt and cook until the onion is soft, about 8 minutes. Drain the Jerusalem artichokes and add to the pot along with the bay leaves. Season with salt. Cook, stirring, until the Jerusalem artichokes begin to soften, about 5 minutes. Add the rice and another pinch of salt and stir to coat with the oil. Cook, stirring, for about 2 minutes to toast the rice.

Add 1 ladleful of the hot chicken stock, stirring constantly over medium to medium-high heat; the mixture should be bubbling. When the rice absorbs the stock and the mixture begins to look dry, add another ladleful, continuing to stir. Cook, stirring constantly and adding 1 ladleful of stock whenever the rice has absorbed the stock, until the rice is creamy and the rice grains are al dente—soft on the outside, with a slight bite in the center—and the Jerusalem artichokes arey very soft. The total cooking time will be about 20 minutes from when the first ladleful of chicken stock is added.

Take the pot off the heat and remove the bay leaves. Quickly stir in the butter and then the grated Parmesan. Taste and adjust the seasoning with salt and pepper. Spoon onto 4 warmed plates and serve immediately. Pass Parmesan for grating and extra-virgin olive oil for drizzling at the table.

farro risotto with broccoli rabe

SERVES 4

5 cups Chicken Stock or or
    Vegetable Stock (pages 208 or
    207) or low-sodium broth
3 tablespoons extra-virgin olive oil,
    plus more for serving
2 cloves garlic, minced
1 small dried red chile or
    ¼ teaspoon crushed red pepper
    flakes
1 large bunch broccoli rabe (about
    1 pound), tough stems
    discarded, coarsely chopped
Kosher salt
1½ cups semipearled farro
Freshly ground pepper
Parmesan cheese, for grating

Nutty farro is cooked here by the method used to make risotto: a fair quantity of simmering stock is added to the farro a small amount at a time so the farro absorbs it slowly and releases its starch. Broccoli rabe, also known as *rapini* or *brocoletti,* resembles turnip greens with a few very small florets among the leaves. It has bitter undertones, but cooking brings out its sweetness. Chicory could also be used in this recipe.

BRING THE STOCK to a simmer in a saucepan. Reduce the heat to very low to keep warm.

Meanwhile, in a large, heavy-bottomed, saucepan, heat 2 tablespoons of the olive oil over medium-high heat until hot but not smoking. Add the garlic and chile and cook until fragrant but not browned, about 30 seconds. Add the broccoli rabe, season with salt, and stir to coat with the oil. Cook until the broccoli rabe begins to wilt, about 2 minutes. Add about ¼ cup of the stock and continue to cook until the broccoli rabe is tender and the liquid has evaporated, about 7 minutes.

Add the remaining 1 tablespoon oil. Stir in the farro. Toast the farro for about 2 minutes, stirring occasionally so it doesn't stick. Add a little hot stock to cover and bring to a simmer, stirring frequently. When all of the stock has been absorbed, add more stock. Continue cooking, adding the stock as it is absorbed, until the farro is tender and nutty, 20 to 25 minutes in all. You may not need to add all of the stock.

Season with salt and pepper. Turn off the heat, cover the pan, and let stand for 2 minutes.

Spoon the farro into warmed bowls and drizzle with olive oil. Offer Parmesan cheese at the table for grating on top.

A 16

Outstanding in the Field Devil's Gulch

24-Jun

Oyster scapece with radishes, fennel, red onions, chiles and mir

Farm egg and new potato frittata with little gems, coppa di testa and b

Grilled
Broccoli rabe with lemon and bottarga
Asparagus with mustard
Carrots with wild watercress and ricotta salata
Spring onions with dried tomatoes and pancetta

Spiedini: pork, rabbit, and lamb

Dessert
Zucchini bread with ricotta, nectarines, honey and black pepper

goat's-milk ricotta and spinach gnocchi

SERVES 4

3 cups whole-milk ricotta,
   preferably goat or sheep

4 ounces spinach

3 large eggs, beaten

¼ to ½ cup unbleached all-purpose
   flour, plus more for dredging

1 teaspoon finely chopped fresh
   marjoram

½ teaspoon kosher salt, or to taste

¼ teaspoon freshly ground pepper,
   or to taste

4 tablespoons unsalted butter

This dish is the perfect showcase for tangy goat's-milk ricotta. If you can't find it, any other whole-milk ricotta will do. An especially good alternative is sheep's-milk ricotta, which is used in Tuscany, where the dish originated. There they call this dish *gnudi,* or "nude," for the gnocchi are essentially ravioli or tortelli filling without a pasta jacket. They are also called *malfati,* or "badly made." The absence of a significant amount of flour makes these gnocchi very light once cooked but also means that forming them is a delicate operation. The key to success is to drain as much liquid as possible from the ricotta so it is very dry before the other ingredients are added.

In fact, I prefer to make these with no flour at all, but finding the driest ricotta necessary for this can be difficult, so adding a little flour makes the cook's work much easier. You may add the full half cup from the start, or add just a quarter cup and then see how easy it is to work with the dough after it has chilled. You can always add the remaining flour then.

Delicate though they are right after cooking, they will firm up by sitting; leftovers are delicious cooked in a few tablespoons of butter until browned on both sides.

SEE PHOTOGRAPH ON PAGE 98.

SPOON THE RICOTTA into the center of a large piece of doubled-over cheesecloth, and tie the ends together tightly with butcher's twine. Tie the bundle to the handle of a wooden spoon and lay the spoon across the top of a bowl deep enough that the ricotta bundle does not touch the bottom. Refrigerate overnight.

Bring a pot of salted water to a boil and prepare a bowl of ice water. Meanwhile, clean the spinach and remove the stems. Add the spinach to the pot and boil for 1 minute. Drain the spinach and transfer it immediately to the ice water to stop the cooking. When the spinach is cool enough to handle, drain it well. Transfer it to a clean dish towel and squeeze out as much water as possible. Chop the spinach very finely.

Squeeze the ricotta bundle firmly to force out all the liquid. The ricotta should be very dry; if you form a tablespoonful into a ball, it should hold its shape. Put the drained ricotta in a medium bowl and add the eggs, spinach, up to $\frac{1}{2}$ cup flour, marjoram, salt, and pepper. Stir well. Cover the bowl and refrigerate for at least 2 hours.

Bring a stockpot of salted water to a boil. Turn the boiling water down so that the water is just barely simmering; there should be very little movement. Pour a generous amount of flour onto a dish.

When ready to cook, scoop out rounded teaspoonfuls of the ricotta mixture and drop several of them onto the flour dish; do not let them touch each other and make sure you have plenty of room around each one to roll it around. When a few gnocchi have been dropped onto the flour, very carefully roll each one in the flour, then gently pick each one up and roll it in your hands to knock off excess flour. Drop the gnocchi into the simmering water. Repeat until all of the gnocchi have been formed and added to the pot.

Turn the heat up so that the water just barely simmers. Cook for 7 minutes. Remove the gnocchi from the water using a mesh skimmer or slotted spoon and divide them among 4 to 6 warmed plates.

Meanwhile, melt the butter over medium heat, swirling gently. Remove the pan from the heat just as the butter begins to foam and turn brown. Pour the warm brown butter on top of the gnocchi. Serve immediately.

pasta with walnut sauce

SERVES 4

1 cup shelled fresh walnuts (from about 7 ounces in the shell)

½ cup whole milk

2 cups cubed crustless fresh bread (2 ounces)

About ⅓ cup Chicken Stock or Vegetable Stock (page 208 or 207) or low-sodium broth

3 tablespoons extra-virgin olive oil, plus more for serving

⅛ teaspoon freshly grated nutmeg

1 clove garlic, pounded with a pinch of salt in a mortar and pestle (optional)

Kosher salt and freshly ground black pepper

1 pound dried pasta, such as spaghetti or penne

Parmesan cheese, for grating

This creamy sauce is supremely subtle and elegant. Peeling the walnuts can be tedious, but the effort makes all the difference; the thin, papery skin on walnut meats can be bitter. If you can, use the season's first walnuts, which are sweeter and less tannic than later walnuts. You may peel them one day in advance. Add the optional raw garlic for a spicy kick or add chopped fresh parsley or basil for flavor and color.

BRING A SMALL POT of water to a boil and add the walnuts. Cook for about 30 seconds, until the skins start to loosen. Drain and pick off as much skin as possible with your fingers, tweezers, or a pin. Don't worry about keeping the walnuts in one piece. You may complete this step up to 1 day in advance; store the walnuts in a tightly sealed container in the refrigerator.

Meanwhile, in a small bowl, pour the milk over the bread and set aside.

Transfer the walnuts to the bowl of a food processor and pulse until they resemble fine bread crumbs. Add the soaked bread and the milk and continue processing. Add the stock until the mixture loosens and looks like a thin hummus. (You may not need to add all of the stock.) Slowly add 3 tablespoons of the olive oil in a steady stream. Blend in the nutmeg, the garlic, if using, and salt and pepper to taste.

Cook the pasta in plenty of boiling salted water until it is tender but still has bite, or al dente. Drain the pasta, reserving about 1 cup of the cooking water.

In a large bowl, toss the pasta with the sauce, adding pasta water as necessary to help moisten and evenly coat the pasta with the sauce. Serve immediately, offering extra-virgin olive oil and Parmesan cheese for grating at the table.

nettle tagliatelle with nettle purée

SERVES 4 TO 6

Long the scourge of hikers and outdoorsfolk of all types, nettles are tamed in this beautiful green pasta with a rich, earthy flavor. It's an ideal way to celebrate the arrival of spring, for this is when nettles are abundant. Use extreme care when handling nettles raw; once cooked, however, they lose their sting.

1 pound wild stinging nettles

About 4 tablespoons extra-virgin olive oil, plus more for serving

3 cups unbleached all-purpose flour, or more if needed

4 large egg yolks

2 large eggs

Kosher salt

1 large onion, diced

1 sprig fresh rosemary

Freshly ground black pepper

Freshly grated Parmesan cheese, for serving (optional)

BRING A STOCKPOT full of salted water to a boil and prepare a bowl of ice water.

Meanwhile, wearing a pair of rubber gloves, clean the nettles and remove any thick stems. Add the nettles to the pot and return to a boil. Boil until the leaves are tender, 1 to 2 minutes. Drain the nettles and plunge them into the ice water. When they are cool enough to handle, drain them, squeezing out any water.

Purée about ⅓ cup of the cooked nettles in a blender until very smooth. Add up to 1 tablespoon olive oil to help them along if they do not blend easily. You should have about ¼ cup purée. Set aside.

To make the pasta dough, mound the flour on a large, clean surface or in a large bowl and make a well in the center. Add the egg yolks, eggs, nettle purée, and a pinch of salt to the well. Mix the wet ingredients with a fork, incorporating a small bit of flour in with each stir. When the mixture begins to come together in a cohesive mass, work with your hands, kneading and turning to form a firm, green dough. The dough should be firm and not sticky; you may not need all of the flour or you may need to work in more. Knead the dough until it is smooth and elastic, 5 to 10 minutes. Pat the dough into a disk and cover it with plastic wrap. Refrigerate it for at least 1 hour.

Cut off about one-quarter of the dough, leaving the rest covered. Flatten the piece of dough well, and run it though the largest setting of a pasta roller. If this is difficult even with a dusting of flour, work with a smaller piece of dough. Fold the piece of dough in three like a letter. Put it back though the roller, the open sides at the top, creating a straight-sided rectangle. Repeat once more to make the dough as straight as possible. If necessary to further straighten the dough, fold it in half crosswise and pass it through the roller, the open side at the top. Reduce the roller size one setting at a time, passing the dough once through each setting, without folding it, until the dough is about 1 millimeter thick. Dust with flour whenever necessary to prevent sticking.

Cut the dough strip into 10-inch-long pieces. Flour each piece and fold it in half crosswise. Cut into ¼-inch-thick strips and toss lightly with your fingers to loosen the noodles. Repeat with the other pieces. Alternatively, use the ¼-inch-wide cutting attachment on your pasta roller. Lay the noodles in a single layer on a baking sheet so they do not to stick together. Roll out the rest of the dough in small batches and cut in the same manner. Set aside.

In a heavy-bottomed skillet, heat 1 tablespoon olive oil over low heat and add the onion, rosemary, and a pinch of salt. Cook, stirring frequently, until the onion is very soft and the mixture is fragrant, about 15 minutes. Add the remaining cooked nettles and continue cooking until very soft, 5 to 10 minutes. Discard the rosemary sprig. Transfer the mixture to a food processor, adding up to 2 tablespoons olive oil to thin it to the consistency of pesto. Season to taste with salt and pepper.

Bring a large pot of salted water to a boil. Add the pasta, return the water to a boil, and boil until al dente, about 2 minutes. Drain the pasta and toss it with the nettle purée. Serve immediately, drizzled with olive oil, and sprinkled with Parmesan cheese, if desired.

smoky sturgeon and potato ravioli

SERVES 4 TO 6

3 cups unbleached all-purpose flour, or more if needed

4 large eggs

½ cup plus 1 teaspoon extra-virgin olive oil

3 medium all-purpose potatoes, such as Yukon Gold, Kennebec, or Yellow Finn (about 8 ounces)

1 large clove garlic, halved

Kosher salt

12 ounces Smoky Grill-Roasted Sturgeon (page 139) or store-bought smoked fish such as trout or mackerel

½ teaspoon fresh lemon juice

6 tablespoons unsalted butter

1 tablespoon fresh thyme leaves

For a dinner honoring Alice Waters at Frog Hollow Farm in Brentwood, California, I visited a sturgeon aquaculture farm in nearby Galt. I returned to the farm with several twenty-pound sturgeon, which we smoked and served in the peach orchard. After that first foray into smoking sturgeon on a farm, we went on to create several dishes using smoked fish, including this one.

TO MAKE THE PASTA DOUGH, mound the flour on a large, clean surface or in a large bowl and make a well in the center. Add the eggs and 1 teaspoon olive oil to the well. Beat the eggs and oil with a fork, incorporating the flour a little at a time. As the mixture comes together, use your hands to work in the flour. The dough should be firm and not sticky; you may not need all of the flour. Knead until the dough is smooth and elastic, 5 to 10 minutes. Pat the dough into a disk and cover with plastic wrap. Set aside to rest at room temperature for 1 hour.

Wash the potatoes and put them into a pot. Cover with salted cold water and bring to a boil. Turn the heat down and simmer until the potatoes can be easily pierced with a knife. Drain. When they are cool enough to handle, peel the potatoes with a paring knife and put them though a ricer or food mill. Set aside.

Put the garlic clove in a mortar and pestle with a pinch of salt and pound it into a paste. Flake the fish into the bowl of a standing electric mixer fitted with the paddle attachment. On high speed, paddle the fish so it breaks up into small pieces. Add the potatoes and the garlic. With the mixer on low speed, pour in the ½ cup olive oil in a slow, steady stream. The mixture should be a creamy but firm paste and hold its shape. Do not overbeat. Add the lemon juice, and salt to taste. If you wish to pipe the filling, put the mixture into a pastry bag fitted with a round ½-inch tip or into a large zippered plastic bag. Set aside.

Prepare a large area on which to make the ravioli. Line 2 sheet pans with parchment paper and dust them with flour; set them aside. Cut off about one-quarter of the pasta; keep the rest covered. Form the dough into a rectangle, and then run it through the largest opening of a pasta roller. Fold the piece of dough in thirds, like a letter. Put it back though the roller, the open ends at the top, creating a straight-sided rectangle. Repeat once more to make the dough as straight as possible. If necessary to further straighten the dough, fold it in half crosswise and pass it through the roller, the open side at the top. Reduce the roller size one setting at a time and pass the dough once through each setting, without folding it. Dust with flour whenever necessary to prevent sticking. You will have a very long, thin sheet of dough that is about 5 inches wide.

Lay the sheet out on the counter and cut it into 2 equal pieces. On one of the sheets, pipe or spoon 1-teaspoon mounds of the sturgeon mixture spaced 1 inch apart. When you have filled the sheet, use a pastry brush or your finger to lightly moisten the exposed dough areas with water. Pick up the reserved pasta sheet and line up one of its short ends evenly with one short end of the bottom layer. Gently press the two layers together at this one edge, and then move slowly up the rows, still holding the top layer in one hand and carefully easing it over each mound of filling. Push out all the air before pressing the two sheets together around each mound, sealing in the filling completely. Using a pasta cutter or a sharp knife, cut between the mounds of filling to form squares. Trim the edges to $\frac{1}{2}$ inch on all sides. Arrange the ravioli in a single layer on the prepared sheet pans. Store the ravioli in the refrigerator while you roll out and fill the rest of the pasta dough.

To cook the ravioli, bring a stockpot of generously salted water to a boil. In a large skillet, heat the butter until it melts and starts to bubble. Add the thyme leaves and remove from the heat. Drop the ravioli into the boiling water, being careful not to overcrowd the pan; you may need to cook the ravioli in batches. Cook until the edges are tender to the touch and the ravioli float to the top, 4 to 6 minutes.

Put the pan of butter back on the heat. Remove the ravioli from the pot with a strainer and put them into the pan of butter with about $\frac{1}{2}$ cup of the pasta cooking water. Swirl the pan so the butter and pasta water combine to make a sauce. Divide the ravioli among 4 to 6 warmed plates and drizzle the sauce on top. Eat immediately.

fish and shellfish

ALBACORE TUNA WITH PRESERVED LEMON AND OLIVE RELISH

———

SLASHED STRIPED BASS FILLETS WITH HERBS

———

POACHED PETRALE SOLE WITH NEW POTATOES, GREEN GARLIC,

AND WATERCRESS PURÉE

———

SALT-CRUSTED WHOLE ROAST SALMON WITH SALSA VERDE

———

SWORDFISH WITH KALE AND ANCHOVY SAUCE

———

BLACK COD WRAPPED IN FIG LEAVES WITH GRILLED SUMMER SQUASH

———

PICKLED TROUT WITH MARINATED ROASTED BEETS AND HORSERADISH CREAM

———

WILD MUSSELS WITH SEA BEANS

———

SPOT PRAWNS WITH CHICKPEA PURÉE

———

SMOKY GRILL-ROASTED STURGEON

———

SEA SCALLOPS WITH SUGAR SNAP PEAS AND CHERVIL

———

RED WINE–BRAISED OCTOPUS WITH ESCAROLE AND CHICKPEAS

albacore tuna with preserved lemon and olive relish

SERVES 4

Albacore is a mild member of the tuna family with light-colored flesh. If you can't find it, any tuna or swordfish steak can be cooked in this way and will be beautifully complemented by the tangy relish.

SEE PHOTOGRAPH ON PAGE 118.

1 whole preserved lemon (page 205)

¼ cup niçoise, kalamata, or taggiasca black olives, pitted and coarsely chopped

1 shallot, minced

1 teaspoon fresh lemon juice

4 (1-inch-thick) albacore tuna steaks (1½ to 2 pounds total)

Kosher salt and freshly ground black pepper

2 to 3 tablespoons vegetable oil

¼ cup fresh flat-leaf parsley leaves

1 tablespoon extra-virgin olive oil

TO MAKE THE RELISH, rinse the lemon under cold water to remove any excess salt. Remove the peel from the flesh and use a knife to scrape any pith from the peel. Cut the peel into very thin 1-inch-long strips. In a small bowl, stir together the peel, olives, shallot, and lemon juice. Set aside.

Season the tuna steaks with salt and pepper. Heat the vegetable oil in a large, heavy-bottomed skillet over medium-high heat until hot but not smoking. Place each of the steaks gently in the pan and cook until nicely browned and crisp, about 2 minutes. Flip the steaks and cook until they are nicely browned and crisp on the other side and their centers are still pink, about 2 minutes.

While the fish is cooking, coarsely chop the parsley. Mix it into the relish mixture along with the extra-virgin olive oil.

Place a tuna steak on each of 4 warmed plates. Top with the relish and serve.

slashed striped bass fillets with herbs

SERVES 6

½ cup packed fresh flat-leaf
    parsley leaves
¼ cup packed fresh chervil leaves
¼ cup packed fresh mint leaves
1 tablespoon fresh thyme leaves
¼ to ⅓ cup plus 2 tablespoons
    extra-virgin olive oil
6 (4- to 6-ounce) striped bass
    fillets, skin attached
Kosher salt and freshly ground
    black pepper

For our dinner at Quail Hill Farm in Amagansett, New York, we served striped bass caught off Montauk Point at the far eastern end of Long Island. Montauk Point is the only place where I've ever seen signs posted that read NO SURFING—FISHING ONLY. Farmed striped bass tend to be of uniform size and are often sold whole. Wild striped bass are available when in season locally; they are much larger than farmed striped bass and because of this they are usually sold filleted.

Striped bass are most common on the East Coast; California white sea bass, which range from California to Alaska, are a good substitution. For this recipe a simple technique provides extraordinary results: a beautiful dish in which the fresh herbs infuse an already tasty fish with even more flavor.

HEAT THE OVEN to 400°F.

Using a sharp knife and working in batches, chop the parsley, chervil, mint, and thyme finely but not so they are completely pulverized. Mix the chopped herbs with enough oil—¼ to ⅓ cup—to make a loose paste. Set aside.

Place the bass fillets, skin side up, on a work surface. Using a sharp knife, score the skin in a crosshatch pattern, making ⅛-inch-deep slashes and spacing them about ½ inch apart. Pat the fillets dry and season with salt and pepper.

Heat the remaining 2 tablespoons olive oil in a large, heavy-bottomed, ovenproof skillet over medium-high heat (you may need 2 skillets to fit all of the fish). When the oil is hot but not smoking, add the bass fillets, skin side down. Cook the fish until the skin is browned and crisp, about 3 minutes per side. Flip the fillets and, working quickly, spread some of the herb paste over the skin and into the slashes of each fillet. Transfer the pan to the oven and bake until the fillets are just opaque throughout, about 5 minutes.

Serve the fish, skin side up, on warmed plates.

poached petrale sole with new potatoes, green garlic, and watercress purée

Petrale sole is a Pacific flounder; use whatever mild sole or flounder is available. This supremely elegant dish is deceptively simple to prepare, making it great for company. Both the potatoes and the tangy watercress purée can be made in advance, and then the finishing steps can be done just before serving.

1 pound small new potatoes

1 fresh or dried bay leaf

1 bunch of watercress (about 7 ounces)

2½ cups Fish Stock or Vegetable Stock (pages 209 or 207) or low-sodium broth

¼ cup extra-virgin olive oil

Kosher salt

4 tablespoons unsalted butter

1 stalk new green garlic

4 to 8 petrale sole, lemon sole, or flounder fillets (about 1½ pounds total)

Freshly ground black pepper

SCRUB THE POTATOES well and place them in a medium saucepan with the bay leaf. Cover with salted cold water and bring to a boil over medium-high heat. Reduce the heat and simmer so the skins will stay intact and the potatoes won't become waterlogged. Cook the potatoes until they are tender and can be easily pierced with a knife, about 30 minutes. Drain the potatoes and let cool. When they are cool enough to handle, peel the potatoes using a paring knife and cut them in half. Set aside.

Remove and discard any thick stems from the watercress. Bring a pot of salted water to a boil and prepare a large bowl of ice water. Add the watercress to the boiling water and cook for about 1 minute, until tender. Plunge the watercress into the ice water to stop the cooking. When cool, squeeze out the water and put the watercress in a blender. Purée the watercress, adding up to ½ cup of the stock to help it along. When the mixture is the consistency of pesto, slowly pour in the olive oil, blending until well mixed. Add salt to taste and set aside.

Trim off and discard the green top from the green garlic. Split the remaining section in half lengthwise. Rinse under cold running water to remove any dirt particles. Cut across on a slant to slice the garlic into thin shards.

To make the poaching liquid for the sole, melt the butter in a large skillet over medium heat. Add the green garlic and a pinch of salt. Cook, stirring, until fragrant, about 1 minute. Add the remaining stock and swirl to combine. Bring the stock to a boil, then reduce the heat and simmer for about 2 minutes to allow the flavors to meld.

In the meantime, put the watercress purée in a small pot and set over low heat to warm, stirring occasionally.

Pat the sole fillets dry with a paper towel and season with salt and pepper. Gently lay each sole fillet into the poaching liquid and cook until the fish flakes, 1 to 2 minutes per side. Arrange the fish on 4 warmed plates and return the pan to the heat. Add the potatoes to the pan and swirl to coat the potatoes with the sauce. Raise the heat to high and cook until the sauce is thick enough to coat the back of a spoon and the potatoes are warm.

Divide the potatoes among the plates and spoon the sauce on top, being sure each portion includes some green garlic shards. Spoon the warmed watercress purée around the fish. Serve immediately.

salt-crusted whole roast salmon with salsa verde

SERVES 6 TO 8

The salt crust protects the salmon from the high heat of the oven and helps preserve the fish's moisture. This technique is perfect not only for cooking whole fish but also whole chicken or large cuts of meat such as rib roasts. You will need a 3-pound box of kosher salt for this recipe.

6 fresh thyme sprigs

1 whole wild or farmed salmon (about 4 pounds), gutted and scaled

Kosher salt and freshly ground black pepper

¼ cup fennel fronds

3 large egg whites, beaten until frothy

1 lemon

6 anchovy fillets

1 tablespoon extra-virgin olive oil, plus more if needed

1 small shallot, minced

1 cup packed fresh flat-leaf parsley leaves

2 teaspoons fresh rosemary leaves

1 tablespoon capers, drained and chopped

HEAT THE OVEN to 400°F. Line a baking pan or rimmed baking sheet large enough to fit the salmon with parchment paper.

Strip enough leaves from the thyme to make 1 tablespoon; set the leaves aside. Rinse the salmon inside and out and pat dry. Season the cavity with salt and pepper and lay the thyme sprigs and fennel fronds inside.

In a large bowl, stir together 6 cups salt with the egg whites to make a paste. In the bottom of the pan, spread half of the salt paste about the length of the salmon minus the head and tail. Place the salmon on top of the paste. Mound the rest of the salt paste on top of the salmon, leaving the head and tail exposed, and pat down firmly. Place in the oven and roast for about 35 minutes. To test for doneness, poke an instant-read thermometer through the salt crust and into the thickest part of the fish; it should read 130°F. Remove the pan from the oven and let the salmon rest for 10 minutes.

While the salmon is cooking, make the salsa verde: Use a citrus zester or vegetable peeler to remove the zest from the lemon. Chop the zest finely and set aside. Squeeze 1 tablespoon juice from the lemon and set aside. In a mortar and pestle, pound the anchovy fillets into a paste with the oil. Add the lemon juice and mix well to combine.

Transfer the anchovy mixture to a bowl and add the shallot. Combine the parsley, thyme leaves, rosemary, and a pinch of salt in the mortar and pound into a paste, adding olive oil as needed to help loosen the mixture. Add the herb paste to the anchovies and shallots along with the reserved lemon zest and the capers. Mix well and add enough olive oil to bring the salsa verde to the consistency of pesto—not too runny but not a thick paste.

Carefully chip away the salt crust from the salmon and remove the skin. Remove large pieces of the flesh from the bones and place on warmed plates. When the whole skeleton is exposed, lift the tail and pull the bones up toward the head; the entire skeleton should come up in one piece. Then divide the bottom portion of the fish, leaving the skin behind. Top each serving with the salsa and serve.

swordfish with kale and anchovy sauce

5 cloves garlic, minced

10 anchovy fillets, chopped

¾ cup extra-virgin olive oil

1 pound dinosaur kale, also called
   cavolo nero

4 (6-ounce) swordfish steaks

Kosher salt and freshly ground
   black pepper

1 dried red chile, finely chopped, or
   ⅛ teaspoon crushed red pepper
   flakes

SERVES 4

The offshore waters near Santa Cruz are warm enough for swordfish for only a short time every year—the season lasts a mere few weeks off Monterey Bay. Pacific swordfish are much smaller than the Atlantic swordfish often seen in restaurants, but the stocks of the West Coast fish are plentiful, so Seafood Watch (page 129) recommends it over the Atlantic swordfish, whose populations are threatened by overfishing. Yellowfin tuna also makes a good substitution.

We served this dish at a beautiful Indian summer dinner at Route One Farm in Santa Cruz, California. Look for swordfish steaks that are 1 inch thick. The anchovy sauce is very salty, so spoon it sparingly over the finished plates. Offer the rest at the table for your guests to help themselves.

IN A SMALL SAUCEPAN, combine the garlic, anchovies, and ½ cup of the olive oil. Place over extremely low heat so the mixture just barely bubbles. If you cannot get the heat of your stove low enough, place the saucepan inside another pan and set them both on the heat. Cook until the garlic is soft and the anchovies have broken down, about 1 hour.

Bring a pot of salted water to a boil and prepare a bowl of ice water. Meanwhile, clean the kale and strip off and discard the stems, including the tough rib that runs up the leaves. Add the greens to the boiling water and cook until tender, about 2 minutes. Drain the greens and plunge them into the ice water. When the greens are cool, drain well, wrap them in a kitchen towel, and squeeze out the excess water. Roughly chop the leaves into 1-inch pieces.

Season the swordfish steaks with salt and pepper. In a heavy-bottomed skillet, heat 2 tablespoons of the olive oil over medium-high heat until hot but not smoking. Add the swordfish steaks to the pan and cook until just opaque and not at all dry, about 3 minutes per side, depending on how thick the steaks are.

While the swordfish is cooking, heat the remaining 2 tablespoons olive oil in another heavy-bottomed skillet over medium-high heat. Add the chile to the pan and let it begin to sizzle. Add the kale and a pinch of salt, but do not stir. Let it settle for several seconds to crisp. Continue in this way, stirring only occasionally, until the greens are warmed through and crispy, 5 minutes. Season to taste with salt and pepper.

Divide the greens among 4 warmed plates and place the fish slightly aside them. Stir the anchovy sauce, spoon it over the fish and greens, and serve.

Outstanding Fisherman

Although Outstanding in the Field spends most of its time inland, occasionally we venture to the sea to get our feet wet. We've dined on the shores of Portsmouth, New Hampshire; in a sea cave on the California coast; and on Puget Sound. These dinners invariably involve seafood, and planning them requires that we call upon the expertise of our fisherman-in-residence, Hans Haveman. Hans runs H&H Fresh Fish in Santa Cruz, California, with Heidi Rhodes, his partner in life and in business. Hans is an articulate spokesman for seafood's vital health benefits; a passionate champion of responsible, sustainable fishing; and above all, a deeply knowledgeable teacher and advocate for the consumer interested in buying, cooking, and eating more seafood. The conscientious consumer of fish and shellfish should be aware of three key issues: season, locality, and the sustainable health of seafood stocks.

Just as produce is local and seasonal, so are fish and shellfish. Although it seems that shrimp, lobster, crabs, and salmon are naturally available whenever and wherever we want them, true Gulf shrimp, Maine lobster, Maryland soft-shell crabs, and Pacific Northwest salmon each has its own season and locality. The ongoing health of these stocks depends on responsible consumers not demanding them when they are not in season and responsible fishers not obliging whatever demand there is. What consumers *should* demand, in contrast, is less sought-after varieties of fish and shellfish. Seafood is unlike almost every other kind of food production in one key way: It's subject to the whim and fancies of a fickle public. It has become almost inevitable that when a particular species of seafood becomes popular with chefs and consumers, the stock is soon in danger of permanent damage due to overfishing.

For a long time I considered the oft-cited counsel "talk to your fishmonger" about what's fresh ridiculous because so few supermarkets have a knowledgeable professional available for talking. But a wonderful shift is taking place: Increasingly, fishers like Hans and Heidi offer their catch directly to consumers at farmers' markets. As with other fresh food, what the fisher has at the market is the best indication of what's local and in season. In addition, this is a fantastic opportunity to meet the person who actually caught your fish and find out what else he or she is catching that you could be eating.

If you don't have a professional fisher at your local market and if, as is so often the case, it's hard to deduce the provenance of the fish at your local grocery store, the last best option is to check Monterey Bay Aquarium's Seafood Watch program (www.seafoodwatch.org). They produce printed and online guides to healthy seafood stocks that are fished or farmed responsibly. Their regularly updated regional guides indicate what seafood is available in different areas of the United States.

black cod wrapped in fig leaves with grilled summer squash

SERVES 4

We served this dish at Santa Cruz's Thomas Farm, owned by pioneering organic farmer Jerry Thomas. Jerry raises heritage turkeys, numerous fruit trees, and a vast number of interesting vegetables. Hans the fisherman (page 128) brought the fresh black cod, and we chose large leaves from Jerry's stately fig tree. The leaves impart a wonderful fragrant vanilla-fig fragrance to the cod. We served the dish with a Storrs Winery Chardonnay from the nearby Christie Vineyard, whose rows of vines could be seen across the valley.

If you, too, have access to freshly caught black cod, you'll be able to get them small enough to be wrapped in leaves. Most commercially available black cod is quite large and sold already filleted, but you may certainly use rockfish or red snapper fillets or whole sardines in place of the black cod.

4 (6-ounce) black cod fillets or whole fresh sardines, gutted and scaled

Kosher salt and freshly ground black pepper

4 to 8 large fresh fig leaves or grape leaves, or as needed depending on the number of fish

1 pound mixed summer squash

Extra-virgin olive oil

Lemon slices, for serving

SOAK 4 BAMBOO skewers in cold water for about 1 hour; this prevents them from burning while on the grill.

Season the fish on both sides if fillets, and inside and out if whole, with salt and pepper. Run the fig leaves under running water to moisten them. If using black cod fillets: Place each fish on half of a fig leaf. Fold the other half of the leaf over the fish and secure the leaf to itself with a skewer; be careful not to pierce the flesh of the fish. If using whole sardines: Wrap each fish in a fig leaf (the leaf will probably wrap around the fish more than once). When all of the fish are wrapped, pierce one skewer through the center of the back and out the belly of one sardine and then another and another until 3 or 4 sardines are lined up belly to back on one skewer. Repeat until all the sardines are skewered.

Slice the summer squash lengthwise into ¼-inch-thick strips. Brush with olive oil and season with salt.

Prepare a medium-hot grill; the coals should be ashed over, with no visible flame.

Grill the fish until it flakes when prodded with a knife, about 5 minutes per side. Grill the squash until tender and well marked on both sides, about 2 minutes per side.

Carefully remove the skewer from each fish and arrange the fish on a platter. Place the grilled summer squash on the platter and drizzle with olive oil before serving with lemon slices, if desired.

pickled trout with marinated roasted beets and horseradish cream

4 (8- to 12-ounce) whole small
    trout, gutted

3 carrots

1 rib celery, cut into a few pieces

1 onion, quartered

3 thyme sprigs

3 fresh or dried bay leaves

Extra-virgin olive oil, for oiling
    the pan

Kosher salt

2 cups white wine vinegar

1 cup white wine

¼ cup sugar

2 medium shallots, thinly sliced into
    rounds

2 small dried red chiles

2 large strips lemon zest, removed
    with a vegetable peeler

12 black peppercorns

1 (1-inch) piece fresh horseradish,
    peeled

½ cup crème fraîche or sour cream

1 teaspoon fresh lemon juice

Freshly ground black pepper

Marinated Roasted Beets (page 87),
    for serving

SERVES 4 TO 8

I am fond of pairing sweet with sour flavors because the intermingling of these opposing tastes highlights the best qualities of both. Sweet alone can easily be cloying and sour alone can be unpleasant, but put together, each tempers the other. This vivid dish is an example of how well that balance can work. Tart pickled trout is matched with sweet beets marinated in light vinaigrette. A crème fraîche and horseradish sauce adds richness and contrasts beautifully with the sharp vinegar in the other two components.

If you are a fisher, or know one well, this is a great way to get the most out of a whole fish. If, on the other hand, the fish aren't biting or you cannot find whole trout at the store, use 8 thin fillets and proceed with the recipe, omitting the fish bones and covering the vegetables with water to make a light stock.

LAY THE TROUT on a cutting board and, using a sharp thin-bladed knife, cut around the head and across the tail. Make an incision down the length of the fish just above the backbone. Holding the knife parallel to the cutting board, use a sawing motion to release the top fillet from the body in one piece. Repeat on the other side. Set the fillets aside in the refrigerator.

Place the bones and heads in a saucepan and cover with 5 cups cold water. Bring to a boil. Cut up 1 of the carrots and add it to the pan along with the celery, onion, thyme sprigs, and 1 of the bay leaves. Reduce the heat and simmer until the stock has a nice fish flavor, about 45 minutes. Skim off any foam that rises to the top as the stock simmers. Strain the stock though a fine mesh strainer and set aside 3 cups. Reserve the rest for another use; it can be frozen for up to 3 months.

Lightly oil the bottom of a 13 x 9 x 2-inch baking pan. Season the trout fillets with salt and lay them in the pan, skin side up, about 1 inch apart. If you cannot fit them all in a single layer, place the remaining fillets in another baking pan just large enough to hold them in a single layer.

Cut the remaining carrots into thin coins. Place them in a medium saucepan along with the remaining bay leaves, the reserved stock, the vinegar, wine, sugar, shallots, chiles, lemon zest, peppercorns, and 4 teaspoons salt. Bring the pickling mixture to a boil and immediately pour it over the trout fillets. If using two pans, be sure to pour it over both. Leave the pan at room temperature until cool. Cover the pan with plastic wrap and refrigerate overnight.

When ready to serve, finely grate the horseradish and blend it with the crème fraîche, lemon juice, and salt and pepper to taste.

Remove the trout fillets from their pickling liquid and place 1 or 2 on each plate along with some of the pickled carrots and shallots. Place a spoonful of horseradish cream and a few marinated beets alongside the fish, and serve.

wild mussels with sea beans

SERVES 2

2 pounds wild or cultivated mussels

8 ounces sea beans, also called
    samphire or sea asparagus

1 tablespoon extra-virgin olive oil

1 shallot, thinly sliced

Kosher salt

½ cup white wine

Country bread, grilled as for
    bruschetta (page 28), for serving

For an autumn seaside dinner, we asked master for-ager Freddy Menge to harvest Pacific mussels. During the first course, our guests were informed that the second course was going to be delayed, as the mus-sels were still being harvested from the nearby sea cove. A few minutes later, Freddy and his wife, Ellen, were seen in the distance lugging buckets full with the afternoon's harvest. If you would like to forage your own mussels, check the harvesting regulations in your area, as they vary from place to place.

Crisp, salty sea beans, often called samphire, grow spring through fall by the edge of the sea or in brackish, marshy areas. If you don't happen to live near a good source of wild sea beans, they can be found at farmers' markets, grocery stores with good produce departments, or online. Otherwise, replace the sea beans with one bunch of fresh spinach. Add the fresh spinach directly to the shallots, cook until wilted, and proceed as directed.

CLEAN THE MUSSELS under cool running water. Scrub off any sand with a stiff brush and pull out the beards with your fingers. Discard any mussels with cracked shells or that don't close when tapped on the counter.

Bring a pot of unsalted water to a boil. Prepare a bowl of ice water. Add the sea beans to the boiling water and cook for about 1 minute, until tender. Drain and plunge the sea beans into the ice water to stop the cooking. Drain the sea beans well, then cut them into 1-inch pieces and set aside.

In a large pan with a tight-fitting lid, heat the olive oil over medium-low heat. Add the shallot with a pinch of salt and cook, stirring, until soft and golden, about 6 minutes. Add the sea beans and toss to coat with the oil. Add the mussels, the white wine, and a pinch of salt and turn the heat to high. Shake the pan to settle the mussels. Cover the pan and cook until the mussels are just open, 2 to 3 minutes.

Transfer to warmed bowls, discarding any mussels that do not open, and serve with grilled country bread to sop up the juices.

spot prawns with chickpea purée

SERVES 4

2 cups dried chickpeas

1 large onion

1 carrot

2 ribs celery

2 cloves garlic

2 thyme sprigs

Kosher salt and freshly ground black pepper

1 pound head-on prawns or medium to large shrimp

2 tablespoons plus ⅓ cup extra-virgin olive oil, plus more for serving

1 tablespoon tomato paste

2 small dried red chiles

1 lemon

2 fresh or dried bay leaves

With Washington State's forested Lummi Island visible in the distance, we dined on bright red spot prawns at a scenic isthmus on Puget Sound. Spot prawns are native to the cool waters that run from Southern California to Alaska. These and other varieties of wild prawn are only seasonally available. You may use any prawns or medium to large shrimp in this recipe; be sure you have enough so each diner gets 6 to 8 of them.

This dish is admittedly labor-intensive, but the complex flavors that the slow cooking yields are more than worth it. It's a wonderful dish for guests because it is beautiful, impressive, and, best of all, can be prepared in advance and assembled at the last minute. Simmering the prawns slowly in warm oil keeps them very moist.

IN A LARGE BOWL, cover the chickpeas with a generous amount of cold water and leave to soak overnight.

Drain the chickpeas and place them in a large pot. Peel the onion and carrot; cut them in half. Trim the celery; cut it in half. Set aside one half of each of the vegetables for the prawn sauce and add the other halves to the pot. Crush the garlic cloves with the side of a heavy knife and add them with the thyme sprigs to the pot. Add cold water to cover and bring to a boil. Reduce the heat and simmer until the chickpeas are very tender and falling apart, 1 to 2 hours, depending on their size and freshness. Skim off any foam that rises to the top as they cook. When they are done, remove the pot from the heat and add about 1½ teaspoons salt and some black pepper to the water; the cooking liquid should taste like salty seawater. As the chickpeas cool, they will absorb the seasoning.

While the chickpeas are cooking, preheat the oven to 400°F.

Remove the heads from the prawns. Place the prawn heads on a baking sheet; return the prawns to the refrigerator until needed. Roast the prawn heads for 10 minutes.

RECIPE CONTINUES

Transfer them to a large saucepan and cover with 4 cups cold water. Bring to a boil. Reduce the heat and simmer until the stock has a nice prawn flavor, about 45 minutes. Strain the stock and set aside $\frac{1}{2}$ cup for reheating the prawns just before serving. The rest, about $2\frac{1}{2}$ cups, will be used to make the prawn sauce.

To make the prawn sauce, very finely chop the reserved onion, carrot, and celery halves. In a small saucepan, heat 2 tablespoons oil over medium heat until hot but not smoking. Add the chopped vegetables and cook, stirring occasionally, until the vegetables have softened and become golden, about 10 minutes. Add a pinch of salt and the tomato paste. Stir to combine and cook for an additional 3 minutes, until the tomato paste caramelizes and becomes sweet. Add the reserved $2\frac{1}{2}$ cups prawn stock and bring to a boil. Turn the heat down and simmer until the sauce is very flavorful, a nice red-orange color and thick enough to hold its shape when dropped on a plate, about 30 minutes. Strain the sauce through a fine mesh sieve, pressing firmly on the vegetables to extract as much liquid as possible. Season with salt and pepper and set aside.

Lightly crush the chiles with the back of a knife. Using a vegetable peeler, remove 3 large strips of zest from the lemon. Pour $\frac{1}{3}$ cup olive oil into a heavy-bottomed skillet. Place the pan over very low heat and add the chiles, strips of lemon zest, and the bay leaves. Season the prawns (still in their shells) with salt and pepper. Gently lay the prawns in the skillet. They should not sizzle. As the shells begin to turn pink, turn the prawns over and cook on the other side. When cooked, about 5 minutes on each side, transfer the prawns to a baking sheet to cool. Peel the prawns, keeping the tails intact. Using a paring knife, remove the vein from the backs and discard. Set aside.

Remove the vegetables and thyme sprigs from the chickpeas. In a blender, purée the chickpeas with some of their cooking liquid in several batches. The purée should be the consistency of applesauce and not too thick; add more cooking liquid as needed. Season to taste with salt and pepper.

To assemble the dish, heat the chickpea purée and the prawn sauce in separate pans. In another pan, heat the reserved $\frac{1}{2}$ cup prawn stock to a simmer. Drop in the peeled prawns and stir briefly until just warmed though, about 30 seconds. Spoon the chickpea purée onto the center of 4 warmed plates. Arrange the prawns on top and drizzle with the prawn sauce. Drizzle with olive oil and serve.

smoky grill-roasted sturgeon

SERVES 4

4 (6-ounce) sturgeon, trout, or mahi
    mahi fillets
2 tablespoons kosher salt
1 tablespoon brown sugar

Smoking fish can take several hours, but simply grilling it using indirect heat and lots of smoking chips gives delicious, smoky results in much less time. Only a little forethought is required: Salt and refrigerate the fish overnight and soak the chips half an hour before throwing them on the grill. Fish prepared this way can be served a variety of ways: with salads such as the Fresh Shell Bean and Herb Salad (page 45), Haricot Vert and Early Girl Tomato Salad with Summer Savory (page 48), or the Potato, Sweet Chile, and Wild Fennel Salad (page 56); flaked and tossed with Bread Salad with Peppers, Radicchio, and Black Olives (page 52); or in the divine Smoky Sturgeon and Potato Ravioli (page 116).

PUT THE STURGEON in a baking dish or other container large enough to hold the fillets in a single layer. In a small bowl, mix the salt and brown sugar with a fork until well combined. Sprinkle the mixture over the fish and cover the dish with plastic wrap. Refrigerate overnight.

When ready to grill the fish, soak 1 to 2 handfuls wood chips in water for 30 minutes. Drain.

Arrange coals on either side of the grill and place an aluminum dish full of water between the piles. Heat the charcoal until it has a light coating of gray ash. Place the chips directly on the coals and place the grate over the coals.

Remove the fillets from the container and pat dry. Arrange the fillets over the water dish in a single layer; do not overlap. Cover the grill lid and all the vents tightly. Grill until the fish reaches 140°F on an instant-read thermometer, 10 to 25 minutes, depending on the thickness of the fillets.

Remove the fillets from the grill and serve hot, at room temperature, or cold.

sea scallops with sugar snap peas and chervil

SERVES 4 TO 6

Sea scallops are dispersed in the northeastern Atlantic Ocean from Newfoundland to North Carolina. The majority of scallops are collected by dragging heavy chain sweeps across the ocean floor. Diver-harvested scallops, on the other hand, are collected one by one from the ocean by divers. Diver-harvested scallops are less gritty than dragged scallops and diving is a more ecologically friendly way to harvest them. This is a simple preparation for ingredients that don't need much fuss to be delicious.

6 tablespoons extra-virgin olive oil, plus more as needed

1 pound sugar snap peas, strings removed

Kosher salt

2 pounds large sea scallops (20 to 30 scallops in all), tough muscle removed if still attached

Freshly ground black pepper

¼ cup white wine

¼ cup Fish Stock (page 209) or water

4 tablespoons unsalted butter, chilled and cut into small pieces

1 teaspoon finely chopped lemon zest

1 tablespoon coarsely chopped chervil

IN A LARGE, heavy-bottomed nonstick skillet, heat about 2 tablespoons of the olive oil over medium heat until hot but not smoking. Add the sugar snap peas and season with salt. Cook, stirring, until crisp-tender, about 2 minutes. Transfer the snap peas to a plate and set aside.

Wipe out the pan with a paper towel and place it back over medium-high heat with another 2 tablespoons of the oil.

Pat the scallops dry and season them with salt and pepper. Place half of the scallops in the hot pan, being careful not to overcrowd them (you may work in more than 2 batches if necessary). Cook without moving them until they are nicely browned and crisp, 2 to 3 minutes. Flip the scallops and continue cooking on the other side until just cooked through, 2 to 3 minutes. They should be slightly firm to the touch, with a very thin line of pale pink in the center when halved. Transfer the cooked scallops to a warm plate and repeat with the remaining scallops, wiping the pan between batches and adding 2 more tablespoons oil to the pan for each batch.

When all of the scallops are cooked, leave the pan unwiped and add the white wine, stock, and any scallop juices that have accumulated on the plate. Simmer until the liquid has reduced by half, 2 minutes. Over very low heat, add the butter a few pieces at a time, swirling the pan continuously. When all of the butter has been incorporated, swirl in the lemon zest and chervil and season to taste with salt and pepper. Return the sugar snap peas to the pan and stir to coat with the sauce.

Arrange the scallops on 4 warmed plates and divide the sugar snap peas and sauce among them. Serve immediately.

red wine–braised octopus with escarole and chickpeas

SERVES 6

Most octopus is sold almost completely cleaned and frozen, but if you have truly whole octopi, follow the directions for cleaning them below. Baby octopi require either very quick or very slow cooking—anything in between, and they'll be rubbery and tough. Few kinds of seafood can tolerate braising—that is, long, slow cooking in liquid—but baby octopus is definitely one of them. This dish has both a mild sea flavor and a hearty earthiness from the chickpeas and escarole. Like the shore where land meets ocean, the pairing is a triumphant one.

1½ cups dried chickpeas

2 onions

2 cloves garlic

1 sprig rosemary

Kosher salt and freshly ground
    black pepper

2 pounds fresh or frozen defrosted
    baby octopuses

3 tablespoons extra-virgin olive oil

1 carrot, finely diced

1 rib celery, finely diced

2 fresh or dried bay leaves

2 tablespoons tomato paste

2 cups red wine

1 head escarole

RINSE AND PICK over the chickpeas. Put them in a large bowl and cover with a generous amount of cold water. Let soak overnight.

Drain the chickpeas and put them in a medium saucepan. Peel 1 of the onions and cut it in half. Crush the garlic cloves with the flat side of a knife. Add the onion, garlic, and rosemary sprig to the pot and cover with cold water by 2 inches. Bring to a boil and then reduce the heat. Simmer, skimming off any impurities as they rise to the top, until the chickpeas are tender, 1 to 2 hours. Remove the vegetables and rosemary and season the cooking water with 1½ teaspoons salt and some black pepper; the chickpeas will absorb the seasoning as they cool.

If the octopi are not already cleaned, cut a slit at the base of the head, above the tentacles, and turn the head inside out. Pull out and discard the intestines and ink sac. Rinse well under running water, then turn right side out and cut the eyes out. At the center of the body is a hard beak; push it out and cut it off if necessary. Rinse the octopi under cold water to remove any sand. Cut them into 1½-inch pieces. Peel the remaining onion and cut it lengthwise in half. Cut off the top and stem of the onion and then thinly slice lengthwise.

Heat 2 tablespoons of the olive oil in a Dutch oven over medium-low heat. Add the onion with a pinch of salt and cook, stirring occasionally, until the onion is soft and translucent, about 8 minutes. Add the carrot, celery, and bay leaves and cook until the carrot and celery are tender, about 5 minutes. Stir in the tomato paste and cook for another 5 minutes, stirring occasionally, until the tomato paste caramelizes and becomes sweet. Add the octopi and season with salt and pepper. Stir to coat the octopi with the tomato paste and vegetables. Pour in the red wine, raise the heat to medium-high, and simmer rapidly until the wine is reduced by half, about 10 minutes Add 4 cups water to cover. Bring to a boil and reduce the heat. Simmer, covered, until the octopi are tender and can be easily pierced with a skewer, 45 minutes to 1 hour. The sauce should be like a thick gravy. If it is still too liquidy, turn up the heat, uncover the pot, and reduce the sauce to the correct consistency. Keep warm.

When the octopi are almost done, warm the chickpeas and a little of their cooking liquid in a pot over medium heat.

Meanwhile, separate the escarole leaves and wash them well. Tear any larger leaves in half. Heat the remaining tablespoon olive oil in a large skillet over medium heat. Add the escarole and season with salt and pepper. Add a splash of water if necessary to help create steam. Cook, stirring frequently, until the leaves are wilted and tender, about 6 minutes.

Divide the chickpeas among 6 warm, shallow bowls. Spoon the octopi and sauce on top and serve with the cooked escarole.

Wineries Across America

One benefit of the explosion of wine awareness in the United States is that many people have a decent wine shop nearby with wines from all over the world. While I think this is a great development, I don't want to overlook the increasing amount of interesting wine being made across America, and the local wine shop is not always the best place to discover these newcomers. Small vineyards are popping up in places both familiar and unusual, but the wine they produce is more likely to show up on the menus of enterprising local restaurants than on shop shelves. The best place by far to taste most of these is directly at the wineries or vineyards themselves.

Without our resident wine guru, Katy Oursler, there would be no Outstanding in the Field, so I begin with one of her favorite regions, the Finger Lakes. With close to one hundred wineries, the Finger Lakes is New York's largest wine-producing region, growing virtually every variety of wine grape. The area is host to one of my favorite American wineries, Silver Thread Vineyard, where winemaker and owner Richard Figiel uses sustainable methods to farm his grapes without chemical pesticides or fertilizers and produces his wine by low-tech means, without electrical refrigeration and with water gravity-fed to the winery. He produces some of best examples of the wine this region is famous for: burgundy-style Pinot Noirs and dry, minerally Rieslings. A Finger Lakes Pinot Noir goes beautifully with earthy dishes such as Wild Rice Baked with Chicken, Fennel, and Porcini (page 100), and the Riesling with spicy food, fish dishes, or anything deep-fried, such as Salted Cod and Potato Croquettes (page 34).

Although Richard Alfaro is growing the ubiquitous Chardonnay grape at his Alfaro Family Vineyards in Napa Valley, the wine he produces from it is a refreshing alternative to most of the familiar California chardonnay. Alfaro's crisp and minerally Chardonnay is unfiltered, which means you can't see through the glass—a great reminder of the earth from which the wine comes. This is a good accompaniment to any hearty white meat or fish dish, such as Butter Lettuce with Seared Chicken Livers and Radishes (page 47) and Swordfish with Kale and Anchovy Sauce (page 126).

On the East Coast, Channing Daughters Winery was founded by sculptor Warren Channing, and his stunning art is all over the vineyards and tasting room, as much a part of the place as the vines themselves. Channing Daughters is the only Long Island producer who grows the Blaufrankisch grape, which is indeed rare all across the country. This delicious grape, popular across Central Europe and especially in Austria and Hungary, makes a medium-bodied red with soft tannins and slightly spicy, meaty, and peppery flavors. It's great with any creamy dish; try it with Pasta with Walnut Sauce (page 113) and Baked Eggs with Spinach and Cream (page 31).

Considering where they are, it's no surprise that the motto of Alexis Bailly Vineyard in Hastings, Minnesota, is "where the grapes can suffer." They have been producing wine since 1978, but it wasn't until fairly recently that they didn't have to go to extremes to keep their vines alive through the frigid Minnesota winters. The University of Minnesota developed the Frontenac grape, which can survive the extreme cold. The wine it makes is reminiscent of Syrah, with a deep, rich color, and flavors and aromas of red fruit and blackberries. It's especially good with hearty dishes, such as Lamb Kidneys with Stewed Fava Beans and Mint (page 184) and Braised Beef Brisket (page 174).

The hot Texas Hill Country climate is especially well suited to nurture the Sangiovese grape, which produces a big wine full of oak, tar, and earthy qualities that emerge with age. Local winery Flat Creek Estate produces an award-winning blend called Super Texan. This dry red complements hearty meat dishes such as Slow-Roasted Pork Belly with Cannellini Beans (page 162) and Pure Maple Syrup–Braised Short Ribs (page 176).

For our dinner in Athens, Georgia, we were lucky to work with John and Martha Ezzard, whose Tiger Mountain Vineyards are located on the 100-acre farm where John was born. They have carefully chosen the grape varietals best suited to the slopes and altitude of the Southern Blue Ridge Mountains. One of those is the Norton grape, widely believed to be one of the very few wine grapes native to North America. The wines made at Tiger Mountain are charming, and the Norton is a top-notch local wine, crisp with aromas of dark red fruit. Try it with pork or poultry, such as Roasted Pork with Fennel Seed and Herbs (page 170) and Pot-Roasted Free-Range Chicken (page 148).

I have tasted wines from each of the wineries mentioned here, but the list is not by any means complete; the diversity of these wineries and the wines they make just hints at the fullness of what is available across the United States. Check out http://wine.appellationamerica.com, www.allamericanwineries.com or www.weekendwinery.com to find a winery near you. Of course, it's hard to make great wine—and sometimes just as hard to find it at an affordable price. But don't turn up your nose at the possibility of discovering something delicious in your own backyard.

poultry and meat

POT-ROASTED FREE-RANGE CHICKEN

———

CHICKEN SALTIMBOCCA

———

STUFFED TURKEY LEGS AND SPIT-ROASTED TURKEY BREAST

———

DUCK BREAST WITH POMEGRANATE SAUCE

———

GRILLED SQUAB WITH SWEET AND SOUR CHERRIES AND WATERCRESS

———

SAUSAGE-STUFFED WHOLE ROAST QUAIL WITH GRAPE SAUCE

———

SLOW-ROASTED PORK BELLY WITH CANNELLINI BEANS

———

PAN-FRIED PORK LOIN WITH HERBED BREAD CRUMBS

———

CIDER-BRAISED PORK SHOULDER

———

ROASTED PORK WITH FENNEL SEED AND HERBS

———

VEAL CHOPS WITH MUSTARD, CAPERS, AND ENDIVE

———

BRAISED BEEF BRISKET

———

PURE MAPLE SYRUP–BRAISED SHORT RIBS

———

GRASS-FED BEEF SKIRT STEAK

———

LAMB STEW WITH BEETS AND MINT GREMOLATA

———

LAMB KIDNEYS WITH STEWED FAVA BEANS AND MINT

———

FRESH LAMB SAUSAGE

———

STUFFED RABBIT LOIN

pot-roasted
free-range chicken

SERVES 4

While pot-roasting ensures tender and juicy meat, the compromise is usually a soggy exterior. That problem is solved in this recipe; by broiling the chicken for a few minutes just before serving, the skin is gloriously darkened and delightfully crisp. Serve with crusty bread to sop up the flavorful juices.

2 carrots

1 large leek, white part only

2 fennel bulbs, fronds removed

2 cloves garlic

4 (10-ounce) bone-in, skin-on
    chicken legs

Kosher salt and freshly ground
    black pepper

1 tablespoon extra-virgin olive oil

2 fresh or dried bay leaves

½ cup white wine

1 quart Chicken Stock (page 208)
    or low-sodium broth

THINLY SLICE the carrots at a slant. Slice the leek in half lengthwise and rinse it under cold running water to remove any dirt or sand. Slice across at a slant the same thickness as the carrots. Cut the fennel bulbs in half through the base, trim the core, and thinly slice lengthwise. Peel the garlic cloves and crush them with the back of a knife.

Season the chicken with salt and pepper. In a large Dutch oven with a tight-fitting lid, heat the olive oil over medium-high heat to hot but not smoking. Lay the chicken, skin side down, in the pot and cook until browned, 6 to 8 minutes. Turn over and brown on the other side, about 4 minutes. Transfer the chicken to a plate and set aside.

Add the vegetables and the bay leaves to the pot with a pinch of salt and stir to coat with the oil, scraping up any bits from the bottom of the pot. Cook until the vegetables begin to sweat, about 3 minutes. Return the chicken to the pot along with any juices. Pour in the wine and cook for 2 minutes. Pour in the chicken stock and bring to a boil. Reduce the heat and simmer, covered, until the meat is very tender, about 1 hour.

About 10 minutes before the chicken is done, place an oven rack in one of the top slots of the oven and preheat the boiler. Remove the chicken from the pot and place it on a baking tray. Broil the chicken until the skin is crisp and nicely darkened, about 5 minutes.

Meanwhile, increase the heat under the pot and bring the mixture to a boil. Cook, uncovered, until the sauce is concentrated, 4 to 5 minutes. Remove the bay leaves and spoon the vegetables and sauce into 4 warmed bowls. Place the chicken on top. Serve.

chicken saltimbocca

SERVES 4 TO 6

4 (6-ounce) boneless, skinless
    chicken breasts

Kosher salt and freshly ground
    black pepper

8 to 16 thin slices prosciutto

8 fresh sage leaves

1 cup unbleached all-purpose flour

2 tablespoons extra-virgin olive oil,
    plus more as needed

2 tablespoons white wine

½ cup Chicken Stock (page 208) or
    low-sodium broth

2 tablespoons unsalted butter,
    chilled and cut into small pieces

Saltimbocca, also made with veal cutlets, is usually served rolled up with the meat completely enclosing the filling. This has always struck me as a shame because the prosciutto and sage leaves look so lovely when draped over the chicken, as here.

PAT THE CHICKEN breasts dry and cut each one in half crosswise into two smaller, more manageable pieces. Place a half between 2 pieces of plastic wrap and, using a mallet or the back of a heavy cleaver, pound it on the underside to ¼ inch thick. Repeat with the other halves. Line up the pounded chicken on a baking sheet or cutting board and season lightly with salt and pepper. (The prosciutto is salty on its own, so the chicken will not need much seasoning.)

Wrap a piece of prosciutto around each piece of chicken, the two ends meeting on the smooth top side of the chicken. (If the prosciutto slice is too short to reach all the way around, wrap a second full or half slice around the chicken.) Lay a sage leaf across the top where the prosciutto ends meet and secure with a toothpick. Be careful not to tear the sage leaf.

Place the flour in a large, shallow dish. Dredge the chicken in the flour, tapping off any excess.

In a heavy-bottomed skillet, heat the olive oil over medium-high heat. When the oil is hot but not smoking, add 2 or 3 pieces of the chicken, toothpick side down. Cook until the chicken is browned and the prosciutto is crisp, about 4 minutes. Turn over and cook for an additional 3 minutes, until just cooked though. Transfer to a warmed plate to rest. Continue with the remaining chicken, adding about 1 tablespoon oil between each batch if necessary.

When all of the chicken is cooked, pour the white wine into the skillet, followed by the chicken stock. Stir with a wooden spoon, scraping up any bits stuck to the pan. Simmer until the liquid is reduced by one-third, 5 to 6 minutes. Over very low heat, add the butter, 1 piece at a time, and swirl continuously until melted and emulsified.

Gently remove the toothpick from each piece of chicken; if necessary, use tongs or tweezers to twist and pull out the toothpicks. The sage leaf should have adhered to the prosciutto. Pour any juices that have accumulated on the plate into the sauce and swirl to combine. Place 2 pieces of chicken on each of 4 warmed plates and pour the sauce on top. Serve immediately.

stuffed turkey legs and spit-roasted turkey breast

SERVES 8 TO 14

1 (12- to 20-pound) turkey

1 bunch dinosaur kale, also called *cavolo nero*, stems removed

2 ounces pancetta or unsmoked bacon, finely chopped (½ cup)

1 small leek, white and light green parts, finely diced

1 small onion, finely diced

Kosher salt

1 tablespoon chopped fresh sage leaves

5 tablespoons extra-virgin olive oil

Freshly ground black pepper

8 sprigs fresh thyme

4 fresh or dried bay leaves

1 large lemon

½ cup ¼-inch cubed crustless country bread

1 tablespoon unbleached all-purpose flour

1 cup Chicken Stock (page 208) or low-sodium broth

This recipe is a refreshing change from traditional roasted turkey and an absolute showstopper for Thanksgiving, especially when served with Beet and Cranberry Chutney (page 204). An inevitable problem when roasting whole turkey is that the breast is done long before the legs are; this recipe solves that problem and goes one better: By stuffing the legs and spit-roasting the breast, a single bird is transformed into two distinct but complementary dishes. And by putting that rotisserie attachment on your grill to good use, it also frees up a lot of space in the oven, another boon at holiday time. Of course, turkey legs, which are sold separately, can be stuffed and roasted as instructed to make an elegant dish any time at all.

To secure the wings and close the cavity for spit-roasting, you can use butcher's twine or thin wire such as that used to hang pictures. If you use twine, make sure to trim the ends close to the knots so none hangs down and risks catching on fire.

Note that the roasting time for the spit-roasted breast is given in terms of the weight of the *whole* bird. Total roasting time for both legs and breast as well as how many servings this dish will yield depends on the size of the bird. Begin checking the breast on the early end of when you think it will be done, for it can easily overcook.

Rotisserie grills vary according to the manufacturer. The instructions given here are based on an electric rotisserie attachment for a standard 22½-inch kettle charcoal grill; you should defer to the owner's manual for your own rotisserie and grill.

RECIPE CONTINUES

PLACE THE TURKEY on a cutting board. Pull one leg away from the body and use a sharp knife to cut through the skin and flesh where the leg joins the body, keeping the knife pressed close to the body. Once the leg is loosened, continue cutting down toward the back until, when you pull the leg away from the body, the thigh bone pops out of its socket. Then turn the turkey over and cut, following the outline of the thigh, from the spine toward the breast until the full leg is removed. Repeat on the other side. Leave the wings attached to the breast. Set the breast aside in the refrigerator.

Lay one leg on a cutting board with the inner leg facing up. Using a sharp knife, cut down the length of the leg and thigh, following the bone. Pull the flesh apart with your hands and scrape along the length of both bones with the knife until they are freed from the flesh. Once the bones are removed, remove the long, thin white tendons from the leg: Grasp one end of each one at a time and use a sharp thin-bladed knife to scrape the flesh off and pull it out. Repeat with the other leg. Set the legs aside in the refrigerator.

Bring a pot of salted water to a boil, and prepare a bowl of ice water. Add the kale to the boiling water and cook until tender, about 3 minutes. Drain and plunge it into the ice water to stop the cooking. When the kale is cool enough to handle, squeeze out as much water as possible and coarsely chop the leaves. Set aside.

Place a large, heavy-bottomed skillet over medium to medium-high heat. Add the diced pancetta and cook until crisp, about 7 minutes. Pour off all but 1 tablespoon of the fat. Reduce the heat to medium. Add the leek and the onion and a pinch of salt to the pan. Cook, stirring occasionally, until soft and golden, about 8 minutes. Add the sage and cook, stirring, for 2 minutes. Add the kale and cook for 5 minutes to allow the flavors to meld. Set aside to cool.

Heat the oven to 400°F.

Remove the breast from the refrigerator. Pour 2 tablespoons of the olive oil onto the breast and rub it all over. Season with salt and pepper inside the cavity and all over the skin. Starting at the neck end, gently run your fingers between the skin and the flesh of the breast to separate them; be careful not to tear the skin. Place a few sprigs of thyme and 1 bay leaf under the skin on each side of the breast. Score the lemon with a paring knife to release its scent. Place the lemon along with the remaining thyme sprigs and bay leaves in the cavity.

Use thin wire to partially close the open cavity, poking it through the flesh on each side of the cavity and securing the two ends. Alternatively, thread a trussing needle with a long strand of butcher's twine and sew up each side of the cavity. Leave the cavity slightly open at the very center so you can get the spit through it.

To secure the wings, poke one end of the wire through the tip of one wing, then run it across the breast and poke it through the end of the other wing. Wrap the wire around the underside of the breast and secure the two ends so the wings stay put while cooking on the turning spit. Alternatively, push the threaded trussing needle through the tip of one wing and then straight through the body and the opposite wing. Then push the needle back through the body very close to the wing all the way to the first side. Tie off the ends securely to hold the wings close to the body.

Push the spit through the tail end lengthwise through the body. Insert the holding prongs into either end and tighten them in place. Secure the breast to the spit as instructed by the manufacturer of the rotisserie. Set the breast aside at room temperature while you stuff the legs and prepare the grill.

Attach the rotisserie base to the grill and arrange the coals on one side of the grill. Place a disposable aluminum drip pan on the bottom grate, centered so that the turkey drippings will fall into it. Light the coals for a hot fire.

Toss the bread cubes with 1 tablespoon of the olive oil and spread them on a baking pan. Toast them in the oven until golden, about 10 minutes. Add the toasted bread to the kale mixture and mix well to combine.

Reduce the oven temperature to 375°F.

Remove the turkey legs from the refrigerator and lay them on a work surface, skin side down and with one of the narrow ends (usually the leg end, from which you removed the tendons) closer to you. Season them with salt and pepper. Divide the kale stuffing between the legs and spread it across each leg, about a third of the way from the end closer to you. Roll the meat away from you into a cylinder. Tie the legs with butcher's twine in about 4 places, like a roast. To prevent the stuffing from falling out the ends when the stuffed legs are cooked, thread a wooden or bamboo skewer through each end to close the opening. Break off the ends of each skewer so the skewer does not extend beyond the meat and the stuffed legs can be easily turned onto all sides. Set the stuffed legs aside.

RECIPE CONTINUES

When the coals are glowing red, attach the spit to the grill and adjust the counterweights so the breast turns evenly. Arrange the drip pan so it is under the breast. Close the cover and turn on the rotisserie. Roast the turkey until it reaches 165°F on an instant-read thermometer and the skin is crispy, 3 to 5 minutes per pound of *whole* turkey. Start checking the turkey at the early end of cooking, as the breast can overcook and dry out quickly. Add more coals if necessary to keep the heat even. Remove the turkey breast from the spit and set it in a warm place to rest for 20 minutes.

As soon as you have put the breast on the grill, cook the legs: In a heavy-bottomed ovenproof skillet, heat the remaining 2 tablespoons olive oil over medium-high heat until hot but not smoking. Add the turkey legs and brown on all sides, 10 to 15 minutes. Transfer the pan to the oven and roast the legs until they reach 175°F on an instant-read thermometer and the skin is crispy, about 1 hour. Remove the legs from the pan and set them aside to rest.

Remove some but not all of the rendered fat in the pan. Add the flour to the pan and cook until it is fragrant and smells toasty, about 5 minutes. Add the stock and any juices from the resting legs and bring to a boil. Boil for 2 minutes and then season with salt and pepper. Pour into a warm gravy boat.

Remove the wings from the breast and place them on a warmed platter. Use a sharp knife to remove the entire breast from the bone and lay it, skin side up, on a cutting board. Slice the breast crosswise into ¼-inch slices and place them on the platter. Remove the butcher's twine from the turkey legs and slice them in ½-inch slices. Arrange on the platter and serve with the sauce.

duck breast with pomegranate sauce

SERVES 6

This well-balanced dish pairs rich, crispy-skinned duck with the sweet-sour juice and jewel-like seeds of pomegranates.

1 pomegranate

4 (8- to 12-ounce) boneless, skin-on
    duck breasts

Kosher salt and freshly ground
    black pepper

½ cup Chicken Stock (page 208) or
    low-sodium broth

1 medium shallot, minced

½ cup pomegranate juice

1 teaspoon sugar

CUT THE POMEGRANATE in half through the stem. Fill a large bowl with water. Holding the pomegranate under the water, remove the seeds with your hands. Drain the seeds well. Set ¼ cup aside. Reserve the rest for another use.

Lay the duck breasts, skin side up, on a cutting board. Using a sharp knife, score the skin in a crosshatch pattern. Be careful to cut into the skin only—not so far that the meat is exposed. Season the duck breasts on both sides with salt and pepper.

Place two heavy-bottomed skillets on medium heat. Lay the duck breasts, skin side down, in the hot pans. Cook slowly until the skin is crisp, about 7 minutes, pouring off any rendered fat into a bowl as the duck cooks. Flip the duck breasts over and cook to medium rare, 5 to 7 minutes. Transfer to a warm plate, skin side up, and set aside to rest.

Pour off all of the fat from one of the skillets and pour in the chicken stock. Place the skillet over medium heat and scrape the bottom of the pan to loosen all the bits stuck there. When all of the bits have been loosened, remove the skillet from the heat and set aside.

Place the other skillet over medium-low heat and add 2 tablespoons of the reserved fat. Add the shallot and a pinch of salt and cook, stirring frequently, until soft and golden, about 6 minutes. Scrape up any bits from the bottom of the pan. Add the pomegranate juice and the sugar and simmer until reduced by half, 3 to 5 minutes. Pour in the chicken stock and simmer slowly until the sauce has thickened and is flavorful, 8 to 10 minutes.

Meanwhile, slice the duck breasts thinly crosswise at an angle and arrange the slices in a fan pattern on 4 warm plates. Pour any meat juices into the sauce, season it with salt and pepper, and add the reserved pomegranate seeds. Spoon the sauce over the duck breasts and serve immediately.

grilled squab with sweet and sour cherries and watercress

SERVES 4

Mild squab is intensified by grilling and well-matched with sweet-sour cherries and peppery watercress.

6 sprigs fresh flat-leaf parsley

2 sprigs fresh sage

1 sprig fresh rosemary

2 tablespoons extra-virgin olive oil,
  plus more for serving

1 tablespoon white wine

4 (1-pound) whole squab

Kosher salt and freshly ground
  pepper

1 small bunch of watercress

1 cup Sweet and Sour Cherries
  (page 196), at room temperature

STRIP THE PARSLEY, sage, and rosemary leaves from their stems and coarsely chop the leaves. In a large bowl or baking dish, mix the herbs with the olive oil and white wine.

Place one squab breast side up on the cutting board with the leg end closer to you, and use a sharp knife or poultry shears to cut straight through the breastbone. Pull the breasts apart to reveal the back and ribs. Cut through where the wing meets the back and ribs, keeping the wing attached to the breast piece; repeat on the other side. Grasp the legs and thighs and bend them sharply down toward the cutting board until the thigh bone pops out of the socket. Cut around the bones and tendons to separate each half from the back and ribs. Be careful, because there is not much more than skin connecting the leg and breast of each half. If necessary, trim away whatever sternum bones are left on the breasts. Repeat with the remaining squab. Add the squab halves to the marinade and turn to coat. Allow to sit at room temperature for 30 minutes.

Prepare a hot grill; the coals should be ashed over and glowing.

Remove the squab from the marinade and pat them dry. Season the squab with salt and pepper and place them, skin side down, on the grill. Grill for about 5 minutes on each side. The skin should be crisp and the breast just firm. Transfer the squab to a warm plate and set aside to rest for about 5 minutes.

Wash the watercress, removing any large, tough stems, and dry it in a salad spinner. Toss with a drizzle of olive oil and season with salt and pepper.

Arrange 2 squab halves on each of 4 warmed plates. Spoon the cherries with a little juice on top and place a few sprigs of watercress on each plate. Serve immediately.

sausage-stuffed whole roast quail with grape sauce

SERVES 4

This is a variation of an Umbrian dish usually made during the wine harvest. Another game bird such as squab, pheasant, or guinea hen can be used; adjust the cooking time for a larger bird. Serve with Beet Greens with Lemon Juice and Extra-Virgin Olive Oil (page 88) or Green Garlic and Potato Gratin (page 96).

4 (4- to 6-ounce) whole quail, preferably partially boned

4 sprigs fresh thyme

Kosher salt and freshly ground black pepper

8 ounces fresh pork or lamb sausage meat

2 tablespoons extra-virgin olive oil

1 large shallot, finely diced

1 pound small seedless red or black grapes, removed from their stems

1 cup Chicken Stock (page 208) or low-sodium broth

STARTING AT the neck end of each quail, use your finger to gently separate the skin from the breast; be careful not to tear the skin. Place a thyme sprig under the skin of each breast. Season the quail inside and out with salt and pepper. Divide the sausage meat into 4 portions and stuff 1 portion into each of the quail. Tie the legs of each quail together to prevent the sausage from coming out during roasting.

Heat the oven to 400°F.

Heat the olive oil in a large ovenproof skillet over medium-high heat until hot but not smoking. Brown the quail on all sides, about 10 minutes. Transfer the pan to the oven and roast until the juices of the quail run clear and their skin is crisp, about 15 minutes. Remove the quail from the oven and set aside on a warmed plate to rest.

Pour off all but 2 tablespoons of the fat from the pan. Place the pan over medium-low heat, add the shallot, and cook until soft, stirring occasionally, about 5 minutes. Add the grapes and stir gently just to coat with the shallot and meat drippings. Pour in the chicken stock and turn the heat to high. Boil until the sauce is thick enough to coat the back of a spoon but the grapes retain their shape, 10 to 12 minutes. Remove from the heat and season with salt and pepper to taste.

Place each quail on a warmed plate and spoon the sauce on top and around.

slow-roasted pork belly with cannellini beans

SERVES 6

The familiar union of pork and beans is rarely as mouthwatering as in this dish. Pork belly is blanched and then roasted so its skin crisps and crackles. The beans are cooked on top of the stove with many fragrant aromatics and then finished in the oven with the pork until both meat and beans are meltingly tender and flavorful. Look for pork belly at farmers' markets or in Asian markets.

3 cups fresh or 1 pound (about
    2 cups) dried cannellini beans
1 (2- to 3-pound) pork belly, skin
    still attached
Kosher salt and freshly ground
    black pepper
4 sprigs fresh sage
2 cloves garlic
½ onion
2 sprigs fresh rosemary

IF USING DRIED BEANS, place them in a large bowl and cover with a generous amount of cold water. Let soak overnight. Drain and rinse the beans.

Fill a medium pot with 1 quart water and bring to a boil.

Meanwhile, using a sharp knife, score the skin of the pork belly in a crosshatch pattern at ½-inch intervals, cutting through the skin to the layer of fat beneath. Set the pork belly on a cutting board in the sink. Pour the boiling water over the pork skin. This will help it to crisp in the oven later. Dry the pork belly with paper towels. Season well with salt and pepper. Stick some sage leaves in the slits of the skin and between any flaps of the meat. Let stand at room temperature for 1 hour.

Crush the garlic with the side of a knife. Put the fresh or soaked dried beans in a large pot with the garlic, onion, rosemary, and remaining sage sprigs and leaves. Add enough cold water to cover by 2 inches. Over medium-high heat, bring to a boil. Reduce the heat, cover, and simmer until just tender, about 30 minutes for fresh beans or 1 to 2 hours for dried beans. Remove the pot from the heat and season the water with 1½ teaspoons salt and some black pepper, or to taste. Allow the beans to cool in their liquid. When cool, strain the beans, reserving ½ cup cooking liquid and discarding the aromatics.

While the beans are cooking, heat the oven to 450°F.

Place the pork belly on a rack in a roasting pan or baking dish. This will allow the fat to run off. Roast the pork in the oven for 30 minutes, until the skin begins to sweat and bubble.

Reduce the oven temperature to 375°F. Roast until the skin darkens and becomes crisp, about 2 hours.

Remove the baking dish from the oven and remove the pork belly and the rack from the pan. Pour off all but 3 tablespoons of the fat. Transfer the strained beans to the roasting pan and add the ½ cup reserved cooking liquid. Rest the pork belly on top of the beans. Return the pan to the oven and roast until the skin of the pork is crisp and hard, 45 minutes to 1 hour.

Place the belly on a carving board to rest for 5 to 10 minutes before carving. Slice, cutting against the grain and leaving a piece of skin crackling attached to each piece. Place a spoonful of beans on each of 6 warmed plates and top with pieces of meat. Serve.

pan-fried pork loin chops with herbed bread crumbs

SERVES 4

Serve these crisp, flavorful chops with a tangy green side dish such as Green Tomato Marmalade (page 194), Beet Greens with Lemon Juice and Extra-Virgin Olive Oil (page 88), Stewed Green Beans (page 86), or a tossed green salad.

4 (6-ounce) boneless pork loin chops
Kosher salt and freshly ground black pepper
2½ cups fresh white bread crumbs (from about 5 cups cubed crustless bread)
1 tablespoon chopped fresh marjoram leaves
1 tablespoon chopped fresh flat-leaf parsley leaves
1 teaspoon chopped fresh rosemary leaves
3 large eggs
½ cup unbleached all-purpose flour
Extra-virgin olive oil

TRIM ALL the fat from the loin chops. Place a chop between 2 pieces of plastic wrap. Using a meat mallet or the side of a heavy cleaver, pound the pork evenly to ¼ inch thick. Repeat with the other chops. Season with salt and pepper and set aside.

Mix the bread crumbs with the marjoram, parsley, and rosemary in a shallow dish. Crack the eggs into another dish and beat together until well combined. Put the flour in a third dish.

Dredge a pounded pork chop in the flour and tap off any excess. Place the chop in the egg and turn it to coat. Finally, lay the pork in the pan of bread crumbs and press the crumbs onto the meat. Transfer the chop to a baking sheet. Repeat with the other chops.

In a large skillet, pour olive oil to a depth of about ½ inch and heat it over medium heat. To test whether the oil is hot enough, toss in a few bread crumbs; the oil is ready if they sizzle immediately. Add 2 pork chops at a time—they will be almost fully submerged in the oil. Cook, flipping them over halfway through cooking, until the bread crumbs are golden and crisp and the meat is done but still juicy, about 7 minutes. Transfer them to a plate lined with paper towels. Cook the remaining chops the same way and serve immediately.

cider-braised pork shoulder

I was moved by the scent of apples to create this dish one crisp autumn day; adding the aroma of slow-braising pork could only be an improvement. Either a picnic shoulder half or Boston butt will work fine here; the skin on the picnic shoulder is a plus for the flavor it adds. The important factor no matter the cut is that it be bone-in, for that adds the most flavor of all. This dish is wonderful accompanied by small turnips and their greens and boiled or roasted potatoes.

1 (3- to 4-pound) bone-in pork
    shoulder half
Kosher salt and freshly ground
    black pepper
4 sprigs fresh sage
2 garlic cloves, slivered
2 tablespoons vegetable oil
1 onion, chopped
1 large carrot, chopped
2 ribs celery, chopped
2 cups hard apple cider
2 cups Pork Stock or Chicken
    Stock (page 210 or 208), or
    low-sodium broth

HEAT THE OVEN to 325°F.

Pat the pork shoulder dry with paper towels and score the skin and fat in a cross-hatch pattern. Season the shoulder well with salt and pepper. Stick a few of the sage leaves in the slits, along with some of the pieces of slivered garlic.

Heat the oil in a heavy-bottomed Dutch oven over medium-high heat to nearly smoking. Add the pork shoulder and brown it well all over, 2 to 3 minutes per side. Transfer the browned shoulder to a plate. Remove any scorched garlic or sage leaves from the pot.

Add the onion, carrot, celery, and remaining sage sprigs to the pot with a pinch of salt and stir, scraping up any bits of meat stuck to the bottom of the pan. Cook, stirring, until the vegetables begin to soften, about 5 minutes. Push the vegetables to one side of the pot and add the remaining garlic to the cleared space. Cook until fragrant, about 30 seconds. Return the pork shoulder and any accumulated juices to the pot and pour the cider and stock on top. Raise the heat to high, bring the liquid to a boil, then reduce the heat and simmer for about 5 minutes.

Cover the pot with a tight-fitting lid and place it in the oven. Check the pot after 10 to 20 minutes; if the liquid is boiling hard, turn the oven down about 10 degrees. Cook, turning once, until the meat is very tender when pieced with a fork, 2½ to 3 hours.

Remove the pot from the oven and place the meat on a plate. Remove the sage sprigs from the cooking juices and skim off any excessive fat. Pass the cooking juices and vegetables through a food mill and into a bowl. If the sauce looks too liquidy, return it to the pot and boil over medium-high heat until it is reduced to the desired consistency.

Slice the pork shoulder and arrange the slices on a warm serving platter. Pour some of the sauce on top and serve, passing the remaining sauce at the table.

roasted pork with fennel seed and herbs

SERVES 6

A 4-pound bone-in rib roast will have about 6 ribs, and these are often sold "frenched," which means all the meat and tendons have been scraped off the top 2 inches or so of the ribs. This step is not crucial for this recipe, so if your roast has not been frenched, don't worry about it; there will just be a little more meat to nibble off those bones. Practically all of the preparation for this dish is done a day ahead of time, so before your guests arrive all you need to do is bring it up to room temperature. Place it in the oven when they arrive, and the aroma of roasting pork and fennel seed will fill the house. Serve the roast hot with Celery Gratin (page 94) and Apple Spread with Lemon Verbena (page 202) or Sweet and Sour Cherries (page 196).

Alternatively, serve the roast cold with Salsa Verde (page 124) or Lemon Mayonnaise (page 206).

1 (4-pound) bone-in pork rib roast, preferably from the loin end

Extra-virgin olive oil

Kosher salt and freshly ground black pepper

1 tablespoon fennel seed

2 sprigs fresh rosemary

4 sprigs fresh sage

1 cup Pork Stock, Chicken Stock, or Vegetable Stock (page 210, 208, or 207) or low-sodium broth

PAT THE ROAST dry and place it on a cutting board. Using a sharp knife, trim away any excess fat from the meat, leaving about a ¼-inch-thick layer. Starting at the top of the roast (where the ribs are thinner), cut the loin away from the rib bones, running the knife lengthwise down the ribs just until you reach the base. Do not cut all the way through; leave the loin attached to the bones at the base. Rub the roast with olive oil and season with salt and pepper all over, including the inside of the flap between the bone and meat.

Crush the fennel seeds in a mortar or with the back of a knife. Sprinkle the fennel over the roast, rubbing it into any crevices. Stick the rosemary and sage between the bones and loin and, using butcher's string, tie up the roast tightly, securing the bone to the loin. Cover loosely and refrigerate for at least 8 hours or overnight.

Remove the roast from the refrigerator 1 hour before cooking to allow the meat to come up to room temperature.

Heat the oven to 375°F.

Place the roast on a wire rack placed over a roasting pan or baking dish. Roast until the meat reaches 140°F on an instant-read thermometer, 1 to 1¼ hours, turning the roast a few times during cooking. This temperature will produce a nice pink color, and the roast will stay very moist. If you prefer the meat less rosy, cook it a few minutes longer, but don't let it rise above 150°F or it will be very dry.

Remove the roast from the oven and transfer it to a plate. Allow the roast to rest in a warm place for 10 to 15 minutes. The temperature will rise 5°F to 10°F degrees as it rests.

Pour off any fat from the roasting pan and place the pan over medium-low heat. Add the stock and scrape up any meat bits from the bottom of the pan. Simmer until the sauce has a nice rich flavor, 5 to 8 minutes. Adjust the seasoning with salt and pepper if necessary.

Place the roast on a cutting board and remove the butcher's string. Remove the herbs and cut the loin off the rib bone. If desired, separate the ribs by cutting between each one and serve them along with the loin. Carve the loin into ⅛- to ¼-inch-thick slices and place them on a warmed platter or individual plates. Pour the sauce on top and serve immediately.

veal chops with mustard, capers, and endive

SERVES 4

2 large heads endive

4 (10- to 12-ounce) veal rib or loin
   chops, each 1 inch thick

Kosher salt and freshly ground
   black pepper

3 tablespoon extra-virgin olive oil

1 small shallot, minced

½ cup Chicken Stock (page 208) or
   low-sodium broth

1 tablespoon spicy brown mustard

2 tablespoons capers, drained

1 tablespoon chopped fresh flat leaf
   parsley leaves

1 teaspoon fresh lemon juice

Veal chops can come from either the rib or the loin. Chops from the rib have a long curved bone, and ones from the loin have a classic T-bone running through the middle. Loin chops are meatier and often more expensive than rib chops. Either is delicious pan-fried, as in this recipe, so buy whichever you prefer.

This dish contrasts different textures to great effect by using complementary flavors in each component: pairing seared veal chops and a hot mustard–caper sauce with a cool, crunchy salad of fresh endive, parsley, and lemon juice.

TRIM THE BOTTOMS off of the endives. Separate the leaves, put them in a bowl, and set aside.

Pat the veal chops dry and season them with salt and pepper. In a large heavy-bottomed skillet, heat 2 tablespoons of the olive oil over medium-high heat until hot but not smoking. Place the veal chops in the pan and cook until browned, about 5 minutes. Turn over the chops and cook for about 5 minutes, or until an instant-read thermometer inserted in the center of a chop reads 140°F for medium-rare to medium. Transfer the chops to a warmed plate to rest.

Add the shallot to the pan and cook, stirring occasionally, until golden, 1 to 2 minutes. Add the stock, mustard, and capers and swirl the pan to combine. Add any juices that have collected on the plate as the veal has rested. Bring the mixture to a boil and cook until thickened slightly, about 2 minutes.

Toss the endive with the parsley, lemon juice, and remaining 1 tablespoon olive oil. Season to taste with salt and pepper and arrange the endive on 4 plates. Place the veal chop alongside the endive and pour the sauce on top. Serve immediately.

braised beef brisket

SERVES 6 TO 8

Beef brisket is a wonderful choice for braising because the long, slow cooking in liquid tenderizes this tough cut of meat. A whole brisket, which comes from the breast, is usually divided into two different cuts: the flat half, also called the first or thin cut, is the more commonly available of the two cuts. It is leaner and thinner than the second cut, which is also called the point, front, or thick cut. If your brisket is from the second cut, it will cook a little longer than indicated in this recipe. Whichever cut you use, make sure your brisket is fresh, and not pickled, brined, or corned.

1 (4- to 5-pound) well-marbled beef
    brisket
Kosher salt and freshly ground
    black pepper
1 tablespoon extra-virgin olive oil
1 large onion, chopped
1 carrot, chopped
2 ribs celery, chopped
1 leek, white part only, chopped
2 sprigs fresh rosemary
2 cloves garlic, minced
2 tablespoons tomato paste
½ cup balsamic vinegar
1 cup red wine

USING A SHARP KNIFE, trim off any excess fat from the brisket; trim the fat cap to about ⅓ inch. Season the meat generously with salt and pepper. Place in a dish, cover, and refrigerate overnight.

Heat the oven to 325°F.

Heat the olive oil in a Dutch oven over medium-high heat (or if the meat is too large to fit in the Dutch oven, cut it in half or use a roasting pan). Add the meat to the pot, fat side down, and brown it on all sides, 10 minutes. Remove the meat to a plate. Pour off all but 2 tablespoons of the fat from the pot.

Add the onion, carrot, celery, and leek to the pot with a pinch of salt. Stir to combine, scraping up any bits from the bottom of the pan. Strip the rosemary leaves from the stems and add the leaves to the pot. Cook, stirring occasionally, until the vegetables soften slightly, about 5 minutes. Move the vegetables to one side of the pot and add the garlic to the clear side. Cook, stirring frequently, until fragrant, about 30 seconds. Add the tomato paste and stir to coat the vegetables. Cook until the tomato paste caramelizes and becomes sweet, about 2 minutes.

Pour in the vinegar and the wine and simmer gently until the liquid is reduced by half, about 10 minutes. Add the meat and any of its juices back to the pan. Add water just to cover and bring the mixture to a boil. Cover the pot with a tight-fitting lid and place in the oven. Check the pot after 10 to 20 minutes; if the liquid is boiling hard, turn the oven down about 10 degrees. Cook, turning once, until the meat is very tender when pierced with a fork, 3 to 4 hours.

Remove the meat from the pot and set aside on a plate to keep warm. Place a food mill over a bowl and pour in the cooking juices and vegetables. Mill the sauce. If it is too thin, simmer the sauce over medium heat to reduce it to the desired consistency. Adjust the seasoning with salt and pepper as necessary. Slice the brisket at an angle against the grain into ½-inch slices and arrange them on a warm platter or plates. Spoon the sauce over the top and serve.

pure maple
syrup–braised
short ribs

SERVES 4

Meltingly tender and with just the right touch of sweetness, these braised ribs are best served with soft
polenta or boiled potatoes. Flanken-style short ribs
are cut across the rib bones, giving long slabs of meat
with four or five short rib bones along the bottom. For
this recipe, those bones should be about 2 inches
long. Ask the butcher to cut 1½- to 2-inch slabs if
those wrapped for sale are narrower than this. Serve
with Green Garlic and Potato Gratin (page 96).

2 to 3 pounds bone-in flanken-style
    short ribs
Kosher salt and freshly ground
    black pepper
2 tablespoons vegetable oil
1 large onion, halved and sliced
1 medium fennel bulb, finely
    chopped
1 carrot, finely chopped
1 fresh or dried bay leaf
2 cups Beef Stock, Chicken Stock,
    or Vegetable Stock (page 211,
    208, or 207) or low-sodium broth
½ cup pure maple syrup

REMOVE ANY excess fat from the short ribs,
leaving the silverskin intact around the bones.
Season well on all sides with salt and pepper,
cover, and refrigerate for 8 to 12 hours.

Heat the oven to 325°F.

Heat the oil in a Dutch oven over medium-
high heat until hot but not smoking. Dry the short ribs with paper towels and brown in the
hot oil on all sides, working in batches if necessary. Reduce the heat to medium if the
bottom of the pan begins to scorch. Transfer the meat to a plate and set aside.

Pour off all but 2 tablespoons of the fat from the pot. Add the onion, fennel, carrot,
bay leaf, and a pinch of salt and pepper, scraping up any meat bits from the bottom of
the pot, cook, stirring occasionally, until the vegetables begin to sweat, about 3 minutes.
Return the short ribs to the pot, bone side down. Pour in the stock and the maple syrup
and bring to a boil. Cover the pot with a lid or aluminum foil and place in the oven. Check
the pot after 10 to 20 minutes; if the liquid is boiling hard, return the oven temperature
about 10 degrees. Cook until the short ribs are very tender when pierced with a fork, 2 to
2½ hours, turning the meat a few times during cooking.

Remove the meat from the pot and place on warm plates. Skim any fat from the
braising liquid and discard. If the sauce is still quite thin, simmer it over medium heat to
reduce and thicken the sauce. Spoon the sauce over the short ribs and serve.

Marin Sun Farms,
Point Reyes Station,
California

Over the past several decades, huge demand for American kitchen staples such as beef, chicken, eggs, and milk has led to the mass production of meat, poultry, and dairy—factory farms of living creatures, in essence. While this has long meant plentiful food at affordable prices, the true cost has been enormous. Animals raised in these settings are fed with little regard for their natural diet and by and large are given only foods and medicines meant to boost their growth and production. The producers of these poor animals are caught in a vicious cycle, for livestock fed and housed in unnatural ways is susceptible to illness and so must be medicated with antibiotics to fight off infection. The resulting "food" from these factory farms may look good on the supermarket shelves, but it's a far cry from what our own bodies are designed to consume over a lifetime.

But there is a movement afoot among people who produce meat, poultry, and dairy from animals meant to be raised on pasture. David Evans is one such rancher, and we have been honored to have him host two Outstanding dinners at Marin Sun Farms (www.marinsunfarms.com), his Bay Area ranch. By the time we connected with David for the first time in 2005, I'd already seen my fair share of organic, sustainable farms and ranches and had found beauty and charm—not to mention delicious food—on all of them. But on my first walk with David to visit the cattle grazing one of the pastures on his 2,000-acre ranch, I witnessed a new brand of small farm magic. With a voice barely above a whisper, he called, "Here, girls," and about thirty-five cows ambled straight over to us with a soft rumble, their hooves thudding across the pasture. Even conventional beef producers know that unstressed cattle make better meat; I'd go so far as to say that David's cattle seem downright *happy*. His chickens are more inscrutable but clearly just as well cared for. David is one of a growing number of poultry farmers who employ portable chicken houses. These structures have raised floors and places for the chickens to lay eggs and roost, just like permanent chicken coops. The advantage is that they can be moved by tractor every few days—usually followed by a large flock of strutting chickens—so the flock has fresh pasture during the day and a familiar, safe haven every night.

Until fairly recently, buying direct from producers like David was a luxury reserved for high-end chefs with the means to connect to out-of-the-way ranchers and, just as important, the storage space to deal with hundreds of pounds of meat. Increasingly, however, grass-fed beef and other livestock ranchers and poultry farmers are reaching out directly to consumers, offering to sell somewhat less than hundreds of pounds at a time (although prices are often better if you can dedicate at least part of a large freezer to the cause). It has been nearly a century since American consumers had such direct access to the source of their food. This is not off-the-grid dining; these folks are fully inspected and certified by the U.S. Department of Agriculture. Their production methods—from where the animals are housed to what they are fed to how they are slaughtered—are also transparent to the consumer, and to me that is a great comfort. As for David Evans's products—true to his philosophy that the long-term goal is locally sustained models all across the country, David will not sell his Marin Sun Farms products nationally, but you can visit www.eatwild.com to locate sources of grass-fed livestock and dairy products near you.

grass-fed beef skirt steak with artichoke and asparagus salad

3 lemons

1 pound small artichokes

¼ cup white wine vinegar

2 fresh or dried bay leaves

Kosher salt

8 ounces thin to medium asparagus

1 small shallot, minced

½ cup extra-virgin olive oil, plus more for serving

4 (8-ounce) skirt steaks

Freshly ground black pepper

4 sprigs fresh mint

SERVES 4

The appearance of artichokes and asparagus on farms and at farmers' markets is a sure proclamation that spring has arrived. A salad made of these two tasty vegetables and little else paired with grilled, flavorful beef is an apt celebration.

In general, there is much less fat on grass-fed beef than on grain-fed. It can become unpleasantly tough if overcooked and is best served rare to medium rare. If you like your meat closer to well done, it should be cooked slower so the juices stay in contact with the meat longer. However, skirt steak is a pretty fatty cut no matter whether it's grass- or grain-fed, so it should remain tender.

SEE PHOTOGRAPH ON PAGE 146.

FILL A LARGE BOWL with cold water. Cut 2 of the lemons in half and juice them into the water, tossing in the lemon rinds as well. Remove the tough outer leaves from each of the artichokes so only the tender, light yellow leaves are showing. Use a paring knife to trim the bottom and to peel off the green outer layer from the stem. Trim the top 1 inch from each artichoke. Put each artichoke in the acidulated water as soon as you are finished trimming it.

When all of the artichokes have been trimmed, cut them in half lengthwise and use a spoon to scoop out the furry choke and the tiniest pinkish leaves. Place the cleaned artichokes in a medium saucepan and cover with cold water. Add the vinegar, bay leaves, and about 1½ tablespoons salt; the water should be just slightly less salty than the sea. Place a piece of parchment paper cut to fit just inside the pan over the artichokes, pressing it down so it touches the water. Bring to a boil over medium-high heat. Reduce the heat and simmer until the artichokes can be easily pierced through the heart with a knife, about 30 minutes. Remove the pot from the heat, remove the parchment from the pan, and let cool completely.

Bring a pot of salted water to a boil and prepare a bowl of ice water. Snap the fibrous ends off the asparagus. Add the asparagus to the boiling water and cook until slightly tender but still with good bite, about 1 minute. Drain the asparagus and plunge it into the ice water to stop the cooking and retain the green color. When cool, dry the asparagus on a clean kitchen towel. Cut on a slant into 1½-inch pieces. Set aside.

Juice the remaining lemon and mix with the shallot in a small bowl. Set aside to macerate for 10 minutes. Add a pinch of salt and, whisking constantly, slowly pour in the olive oil. Set the dressing aside.

Remove the artichokes from their cooking liquid and slice them thinly lengthwise from top to stem. Combine the sliced artichokes and the asparagus in a medium bowl and set aside.

Prepare the grill so the coals are glowing red but no flame is visible. Trim any excess fat from the steaks and season them with salt and pepper. Grill for 2 to 4 minutes on each side, depending on their thickness, for medium rare. Set the steaks aside on a warm plate to rest.

Strip the leaves of mint from the stems and coarsely chop the leaves. Put them in the bowl with the artichokes and asparagus. Add the dressing and toss lightly to combine. Season to taste with salt and pepper.

Arrange the salad on 4 plates. Slice the steaks against the grain and on a slant. Arrange the slices of meat on the plates with the salad, pouring any juices on top. Drizzle with olive oil and serve.

lamb stew with beets and mint gremolata

SERVES 4

When I think of lamb, I think of Colorado, and especially of Zephyros Farm, where we have had two Outstanding dinners. Located in the shadow of the Rockies, Zephyros Farm raises grass-fed summer lamb that is some of the best I've ever had.

For this stew, use whichever type of beet you like, but note that red beets will turn the stew bright pink.

1½ pounds boneless lamb shoulder, trimmed of excess fat and cut into 1-inch cubes

Kosher salt and freshly ground black pepper

1 tablespoon extra-virgin olive oil

1 onion, chopped

1 carrot, chopped

1 leek, white part only, chopped

½ cup red wine

4 medium Chioggia, gold, or red beets, peeled and cut into 1-inch-thick wedges

6 sprigs fresh mint

6 sprigs fresh flat-leaf parsley

Grated zest of 1 orange

1 garlic clove, minced

SEASON THE LAMB with salt and pepper. In a Dutch oven or other heavy-bottomed pot, heat the olive oil over medium-high heat. Brown the lamb on all sides, working in batches. Use a slotted spoon to transfer the browned meat to a plate and set aside.

Reduce the heat under the pot to medium-low. Add the onion, carrot, and leek with a pinch of salt, scraping up any browned bits from the bottom. Cook, stirring occasionally, until the vegetables begin to soften, about 4 minutes.

Return the meat and any of its juices to the pot. Stir to combine and pour in the red wine. Increase the heat and simmer briefly until the wine is reduced by half, about 5 minutes. Add the beets and stir to coat them with the juices. Add water to cover and bring to a boil.

Reduce the heat and simmer, covered, for 45 minutes. Remove the lid and continue to cook until the meat is tender, 30 to 45 minutes. The sauce should have reduced to a thick gravy; if it looks too watery, simmer, uncovered, to reduce the sauce to the correct consistency.

Meanwhile, to make the gremolata, remove the mint and parsley leaves from the stems. Chop the herbs finely and place them in a small bowl. Add the orange zest and garlic clove. Mix well and season to taste with salt and pepper.

Serve the stew in warm bowls, topped with the gremolata.

lamb kidneys with stewed fava beans and mint

SERVES 4

6 lamb kidneys (about 1 pound
   total)

1½ cups whole milk

1 pound shelled fresh fava beans
   (from about 3 pounds in the pod)

3 tablespoons extra-virgin olive oil

1 tablespoon unsalted butter

½ onion, finely chopped

Kosher salt

2 sprigs fresh mint

Freshly ground black pepper

1 cup Chicken Stock (page 208) or
   low-sodium broth

½ cup unbleached all-purpose flour

Many of the ranchers and poultry farmers we work with are understandably adamant that most parts of their animals be used once slaughtered. To them, it is the height of wastefulness to consume only the "choice" cuts of meat; eating responsibly is eating as much of a slaughtered animal as possible. For the consumer it's worth seeking out less-favored cuts and organ meat, not only for the reasons espoused by my ranching and farming friends, but also because so much of this meat is delicious, and since it is not so popular, it can usually be had at bargain prices. Lamb kidneys have a milder flavor than beef or pork kidneys. They are also much more tender and so are ideally suited to quick cooking.

PUT THE KIDNEYS in a bowl and pour the milk over them. Cover the bowl and set aside in the refrigerator for 2 hours.

While the kidneys are soaking, bring a pot of salted water to a boil and prepare a bowl of ice water. Cook the fava beans in the boiling water for 1 minute to loosen their skins. Drain the fava beans and plunge immediately in the ice water to stop the cooking process. When the fava beans are cool enough to handle, drain them and then peel off and discard their skins. Set the beans aside.

Heat 1 tablespoon of the olive oil and the butter in a heavy-bottomed, deep skillet over medium-low heat. Add the onion and a pinch of salt. Cook, stirring occasionally, until the onion is soft and translucent, about 8 minutes. Add the fava beans, 1 sprig of the mint, and salt and pepper to taste. Raise the heat to medium, and when the moisture from the favas has evaporated, 1 to 2 minutes, add ½ cup of the chicken stock. Reduce the heat and simmer gently until the beans are soft and beginning to break down, about 10 minutes. Remove and discard the mint sprig and set the skillet aside.

Rinse the kidneys well with cold water and dry gently with paper towels. Cut the kidneys in half lengthwise and remove and discard any fat or membrane. Season the kidneys with salt and pepper and dredge them in the flour, tapping gently to remove the excess. Heat the remaining 2 tablespoons olive oil in a large skillet over medium-high heat until almost smoking. Add the kidneys and cook for about 1 minute on each side. They should be pink in the middle. Transfer the kidneys to a warm plate and set aside to rest.

Pour the remaining ½ cup chicken stock into the pan and simmer over low heat, scraping up any bits of meat on the bottom of the pan. Swirl the pan over the heat until the sauce is slightly reduced, 2 minutes.

Return the pot of fava beans to the burner to reheat. Strip the leaves from the remaining sprig of mint and thinly slice the leaves. Stir the mint into the fava beans.

Divide the fava beans among 4 warmed plates. Top with the lamb kidneys, pour the pan sauce on top, and serve.

fresh lamb sausage

1 pound boneless lamb shoulder,
    cut into 1-inch cubes

8 ounces pork fat, cut into 1-inch
    cubes

2 ounces pancetta or unsmoked
    streaky bacon, finely diced

Kosher salt and freshly ground
    pepper

1 tablespoon extra-virgin olive oil,
    plus more for cooking

1 small onion, minced

1 tablespoon finely chopped fresh
    rosemary leaves

5 to 6 feet of lamb or hog casings
    (optional)

**MAKES ABOUT 8 SAUSAGES;
SERVES 4 TO 6**

It is easy to make sausage at home with just a few pieces of special equipment. The fresh flavor and lack of additives make it well worth the effort. You will need a meat grinder (it is easy to find a model that attaches to your electric stand mixer) equipped with a tray to hold the meat and a plunger to feed it into the grinder. A stuffing attachment with a horn is also needed to feed the meat into the casings, or you may forgo this step and simply form the sausage into patties.

A well-stocked butcher or specialty food shop will have lamb or hog casings, and you can ask the butcher to set aside some fat for you when he trims the pork; most won't even charge you for it.

IN A LARGE BOWL, combine the lamb meat, pork fat, pancetta, 2 teaspoons salt, and a pinch of pepper. Mix well and cover with plastic wrap. Refrigerate for at least 8 hours or overnight.

Place all of the sausage-making equipment and a large bowl in the refrigerator until very cold. This will keep the ingredients cool while they are being ground, and the texture of the sausage will remain coarse and not get mushy.

In a heavy-bottomed skillet, heat the olive oil over medium-low heat. Add the onion, rosemary, and a pinch of salt. Cook slowly, stirring occasionally, until the onion is soft but not at all brown, about 8 minutes. Remove from the heat and let cool completely.

Using a wooden spoon, mix the onion mixture into the meat so it is well distributed. Assemble the grinder. Place the chilled bowl beneath the grinder to catch the ground mixture. Put the meat onto the feeding plate and feed it into the grinder, using the plunger to push it through so it drops into the bowl below.

When all of the meat has been ground, test the seasoning of the sausage by forming a small patty and cooking it in a small skillet. Taste and adjust the seasoning with salt and

RECIPE CONTINUES

pepper as necessary. If you are not going to stuff the sausages into casings, form the ground sausage into patties and cook as for links, below. If you are going to proceed with the stuffing, loosely cover the sausage meat with plastic wrap and return it the refrigerator. Clean all of the grinder attachments and return the stuffing horn and all of the grinder attachments except the grinding knife and plate to the refrigerator.

Rinse the outside of the casing well in cold water. Thread the end onto the faucet spout and run a slow stream of cold water through the casing to rinse out the inside.

Reassemble the grinder and mount the chilled stuffing horn. Slide the casing over the tip of the horn so it forms pleats and the entire length of the casing is over the horn. If the entire length of casing does not fit, cut it in half and work in 2 batches. Place the sausage meat onto the feeding plate and, using the plunger, feed it though the machine at the lowest speed. Just before the meat is exposed through the tip of the horn, turn off the machine, pull forward 2 inches of casing, and tie a knot in the end to keep it closed. Hold the casing in place at the tip of the horn and turn the machine back on to the lowest speed. Gradually release the casing as it is filled with the meat. Stop the machine with at least 5 inches of empty casing remaining. Form the length of sausage into links by pinching it into 4- to 6-inch sections. Twist the links a few times to close, creating a ¼-inch space between them and squeezing the meat at each end to tighten and make the links plump. When you reach the end, tie the remaining casing into a knot. Chill the sausages for at least 8 hours and up to 24 hours before cooking. Remove the sausages from the refrigerator 30 minutes before cooking.

Pour a very thin coating of olive oil in a large skillet and heat over medium-low heat. Prick the sausages with a pin to prevent the casing from bursting. Add the links to the pan and cook until well browned on all sides and slightly pink in the center, about 10 minutes.

Cut into links and serve.

stuffed rabbit loin

SERVES 4

4 (5-ounce) boneless rabbit loins
   with flaps intact

Kosher salt and freshly ground
   black pepper

4 slices prosciutto or Serrano ham

2 rabbit or chicken livers, cut in
   half

2 sprigs fresh thyme

2 tablespoons extra-virgin olive oil

½ cup Chicken Stock (page 208) or
   low-sodium broth

Rabbit loin has a nice, firm texture and pleasant, mild flavor. It is extremely lean, however, so it needs some extra fat to keep it from drying out during cooking. In this dish, prosciutto adds both flavor and fat. Serve with white beans, roasted vegetables, or small boiled potatoes and a slightly sweet accompaniment, such as Sweet and Sour Cherries (page 196) or Beet and Cranberry Chutney (page 204). For a touch of sweetness on the inside, coarsely chop a few pitted prunes and add some to each loin along with the livers.

LAY THE LOINS out on a flat work surface with the thicker ends closer to you. Season the loins with salt and pepper. Fold the prosciutto slices crosswise in half and lay one on each of the loins. Arrange one liver half on top of the prosciutto about 1 inch from the end closer to you, so it rests between the thick and thinner parts of the rabbit loin. Strip the leaves of thyme from the sprigs and sprinkle over the liver and prosciutto. Starting at the end closer to you, roll the loins. Tie the loins like a roast with 2 or 3 pieces of butcher's twine.

Heat the oven to 400°F.

Heat the oil in an ovenproof heavy-bottomed skillet over medium-high heat. Season the loins with salt and pepper and place them in the hot pan, turning to brown on all sides, 5 to 8 minutes. Transfer the pan to the oven and roast the loins until they reach 155°F on an instant-read thermometer, 5 to 7 minutes. Remove the loins from the pan and set them aside on a warm plate.

Place the pan over medium heat and pour in the chicken stock. Simmer until the stock is reduced by half, about 3 minutes. Remove the butcher's twine from the loins and cut them at an angle into ½-inch slices. Arrange the slices on 4 warmed plates and pour the sauce on top. Serve.

extras and a few basics

PICKLED WILD MUSHROOMS

———

GREEN TOMATO MARMALADE

———

SWEET AND SOUR CHERRIES

———

DRIED TOMATO CONSERVE

———

APPLE SPREAD WITH LEMON VERBENA

———

BEET AND CRANBERRY CHUTNEY

———

PRESERVED LEMONS

———

LEMON MAYONNAISE

———

VEGETABLE STOCK

———

CHICKEN STOCK

———

FISH STOCK

———

PORK STOCK

———

BEEF STOCK

pickled wild mushrooms

MAKES 4 PINTS

Serve these tangy mushrooms as part of an appetizer platter with roasted peppers and a selection of salumi. I include here directions for water bath canning; if you have a pressure canner, follow the manufacturer's instructions. Remember that glass canning jars and their metal rings can be reused but that you need to use new lids every time. Alternatively, if you do not want to process the jars, refrigerate them and consume the mushrooms within a few weeks.

SEE PHOTOGRAPH ON PAGE 190.

2 pounds wild mushrooms, such as chanterelles, porcini, or yellowfoot

2 carrots, thinly sliced

3 cups champagne vinegar of at least 5% acidity

1 cup white wine

⅓ cup sugar

2 tablespoons pickling salt

12 black peppercorns

12 coriander seeds

2 large dried chiles, chopped

4 fresh or dried bay leaves

WASH FOUR 1-pint glass canning jars, their rings, and lids in a dishwasher or with hot, soapy water and rinse them thoroughly. Place the jars in the canner (or in a large pot fitted with a metal rack) and cover with hot water. Bring the water to a boil and boil vigorously for 10 minutes. You may leave the jars in the hot water while you prepare the mushrooms.

A few minutes before you are ready to transfer the mushrooms to the jars, pour simmering—not boiling—water over the lids to soften the seal, or follow the manufacturer's instructions for preparing the lids.

Use a damp cloth to wipe any dirt or sand from the mushrooms. Cut any larger mushrooms into halves or quarters; leave them whole if they are a manageable size. Set the mushrooms aside.

Combine the carrots, vinegar, 1 cup water, the sugar, pickling salt, peppercorns, coriander seeds, chiles, and bay leaves in a large pot. Bring the mixture to a boil and then add the mushrooms. Bring the mixture back to a boil, then reduce the heat, and simmer for 5 minutes.

Drain the jars and pack the mushrooms into the hot, sterilized jars, leaving ½ inch headspace at the top of each jar. Pour the hot pickling liquid into the jars to cover the mushrooms. Thoroughly wipe the rims and threads of the jars with a clean, damp cloth.

Set the lids in place and screw on the rings. Any jar that has more than $\frac{1}{2}$ inch headspace should be refrigerated, not processed, and eaten within a couple of weeks.

Fill the canner with hot water and add the jars; the jars should be covered by 1 to 2 inches. Cover the canner and bring the water to a boil. Start timing once the water reaches a boil and process for 10 minutes. Using a jar lifter, remove the jars from the pot and let cool for at least 12 hours in a location without any drafts. To test the seal after this time, press down on the lid; it should not move when pressed.

Set aside in a cool, dry, and dark place for at least 2 weeks before using. The pickled wild mushrooms will keep for up to 1 year. Discard if at any time the mixture looks moldy, foamy, or murky, or if it does not smell right when opened.

green tomato marmalade

MAKES ABOUT 2 CUPS

2 pounds firm, green tomatoes

1 lemon

2 cups sugar

½ teaspoon kosher salt

½ vanilla bean

Vern Stockwell of Stockwell Farm near Palmer, Alaska, is among the most tenacious farmers I've met on the Outstanding tour. We were there in late August and he showed us around his farm, abundant with cabbages, broccoli, and potatoes—all vegetables that grow quite well in the short Alaska season. We came across a greenhouse where, he told us, he'd been trying to grow red tomatoes for several years. Trouble was, more than half of those years the tomatoes never actually turned red. Sure enough, when we poked our heads through the door, the entire greenhouse was full of healthy, very green tomatoes. We met Alaska's August challenge with this recipe; in the rest of the country, it's more likely to be an end-of-season treat. Serve the marmalade with oily fish, grilled or roasted meats, or a strong aged cheese.

CUT THE TOMATOES in half and remove the seeds and core. Chop into small dice.

Use a vegetable peeler to remove the zest from the lemon and cut it in thin strips. Juice the lemon. In a large bowl, combine the tomatoes, lemon zest, lemon juice, sugar, and salt. Cover and refrigerate for 8 hours or overnight.

Put the tomato mixture into a large nonreactive pot. Cut the vanilla bean in half lengthwise and scrape the seeds into the tomato mixture. Add the scraped bean as well. Bring the mixture to a boil, stirring constantly. Lower the heat and simmer until the marmalade has thickened, 2 to 2½ hours. Place a small spoonful on a plate; when cool, the marmalade should not be runny but have a jamlike consistency.

Remove the vanilla bean and let the marmalade cool. Serve at room temperature or chilled. The marmalade can be refrigerated for up to 2 weeks.

sweet and sour cheries

MAKES ABOUT 2 CUPS

These tangy, sweet cherries are delicious with grilled or roasted game birds, such as Grilled Squab (page 158) or duck, or with venison.

¾ cup champagne or white wine vinegar

1 cup sugar

¼ cup kirsch

¼ teaspoon kosher salt

1 pound fresh cherries, pitted

COMBINE THE VINEGAR, sugar, kirsch, and salt in a medium nonreactive saucepan and bring to a boil over medium heat. Lower the heat and simmer, stirring frequently, until the sugar is dissolved, 1 minute. Add the cherries and simmer until they are soft but still hold their shape, about 8 minutes. Cool completely, and then refrigerate for 2 days before serving to allow the flavors to meld and intensify. The cherries will keep for up to 1 week refrigerated.

Boggy Creek Farm,
Austin, Texas

Within Austin city limits lies Boggy Creek Farm, one of the few organic urban farms in the United States. Owned and operated by Larry Butler and Carol Ann Sayle, Boggy Creek Farm is a haven for Austinites who visit twice a week to buy fresh produce and other products, including a neighbor's goat's-milk ice cream, Sweetgrass Dairy cheeses, and Boggy Creek pecans. But those city dwellers and, especially, their children come for more than just food; they come to walk around the fields, pet the chickens, and simply enjoy a visit with Larry and Carol Ann, who are always happy to show guests around and share a recipe or a story.

It's no wonder so many come so often from near and far. With its stately pecan trees and historic mid-1800s farmhouse, this five-acre farm is one of the loveliest we've visited on the Outstanding tour, and those pecan trees certainly provide good cover from the hot Texas sun. Texas summer, steamy enough to make Californians wilt, is why growing seasons are more dramatically delineated here than in other parts of the country. Whereas in many areas summer means growing lettuce and tomatoes at the same time, Larry, Carol Ann, and other Central Texas farmers work with the seasons a little differently, growing kale, lettuce, and other greens during the cooler winter, and tomatoes, squash, and cucumbers during the hottest part of summer.

Like those of many passionate farmers, Larry and Carol Ann's personal pursuits dovetail with their professional farm life. Carol Ann is a painter of beautiful, natural Texas scenes, and Larry's specialty is smoke-drying his own tomatoes right on the farm. Their sweet-tart smokiness is addictive; the heady combination reminds me of Central Texas and its people: assertive and lively, perfect for the Dried Tomato Conserve (page 199) we made for our dinner there.

dried tomato conserve

This pungent condiment goes great with grilled meats or hard aged cheeses. We first made it with Larry Butler's smoke-dried tomatoes (page 197), but I've made it since using regular dried tomatoes, with excellent results.

2 tablespoons extra-virgin olive oil

1 tablespoon unsalted butter

2 large onions, finely diced

1 dried red chile, finely chopped, or ¼ teaspoon crushed red pepper flakes

1 teaspoon finely chopped fresh rosemary leaves

¼ cup sugar

¼ cup red wine

2 tablespoons red wine vinegar

1 cup dried tomatoes, coarsely chopped

Kosher salt and freshly ground black pepper

HEAT THE OIL and butter in a large, heavy-bottomed saucepan over medium heat. When the foaming subsides, add the onions, chile, and rosemary. Cook, stirring, until the onions start to sweat, about 4 minutes. Add the sugar and continue cooking, stirring occasionally, until the onions are soft and golden, 8 to 10 minutes. Add ¼ cup water and the wine, vinegar, and tomatoes along with salt and pepper to taste. Simmer gently over medium-low heat, stirring occasionally, until thick, about 30 minutes. Let cool completely. The conserve can be eaten the day it is made, but the flavors will continue to develop for the better if it sits a few days more. Store in the refrigerator; bring to room temperature before serving.

My Outstanding
Brother, Bill

My oldest brother, Bill, is a pioneering organic apple farmer and consultant in the Santa Cruz Mountains. Bill has farmed organically since 1975 and is one of the longest-standing members of the California Certified Organic Farmers. As a teenager, I occasionally worked in his orchard harvesting apples and pears. Since 1999, we have celebrated four Outstanding dinners in the orchards at Bill's Happy Valley Farm in Santa Cruz. Bill is a good example of the obsessive attention to detail that America's artisanal small orchardists must practice to be successful. Where large-scale industrial fruit growers depend on the wide use of pesticides and uniform, machine-facilitated pruning, Bill employs time-consuming, labor-intensive growing methods. His orchards are primarily low- or nonirrigated, which requires much more maintenance to ensure the health of the trees, and he thoroughly thins his trees by hand, which takes much more time than pruning by machine. But the payoff of these artisanal methods is huge: Bill's trees produce larger, sweeter fruit with bolder flavors than any grown by conventional methods.

Although the growing interest in heirloom varieties of fruits and vegetables is satisfying to farmers and orchardists like Bill, there is a fair amount of misunderstanding about what exactly the term *heirloom* means. *Heirloom* is not in and of itself a taste or texture characteristic, nor does it signify whether the apple is good for eating or best for cooking in pies or making into applesauce or pressing for juice. None of this helpful information for the cook can be gleaned from the word *heirloom*. What the term *does* indicate is that the particular variety of fruit, vegetable, or flower is old—some varieties have been around for hundreds if not thousands of years—and is an open-pollinated cultivar. This means the plant was grown from a seed, and that all previous generations and all subsequent generations of that plant look alike.

Now, for anyone who as a child saved apple seeds or avocado pits, and then planted them and watched plants grow, it may seem elementary that this is how all fruits and vegetables are grown. Industrial farming, however, is nothing like that at all. The produce sold at your local grocery store, by and large, is bred to be sturdy enough to ship across the country or even the world. Cultivars are bred to express the most desirable characteristics (nice color and good durability, for example); some of these are just heartier versions of heirlooms and some are hybrids, wherein two different cultivars are crossed to create a new cultivar. Most hybrids cannot self-germinate, or grow from  seeds, and require human intervention to sprout. In other words, plant a seed from a tomato bought in January—almost definitely a modern hybrid—and it's unlikely anything at all will happen. What modern farming and hybridization have done, essentially, is deemphasize taste and nutrition in a multitude of varieties of fruits, vegetables, and flowers in favor of the resilience of just a few. Paradoxically, however, many modern cultivars are actually less resilient than the hearty heirlooms, which evolved naturally over time to resist diseases, pests, and weather fluctuations.

For the consumer, though, the most exciting aspects of heirlooms may be their fantastic, often complex flavor and their diversity. Instead of the four or five types of apples and two kinds of pears commonly available at the grocery store, Bill grows thirty kinds of heirloom apples and pears, and each is as distinct from the other as are human members of a single family, from the familiar Granny Smith, Red Delicious, and Macintosh to the somewhat less known Newtown Pippin, Mutsu (also known as Crispin), and Pink Pearl. It is worth noting that in spite of all the recent enthusiasm about the resurgence of heirloom produce, not all heirlooms are, or were, created equal, and not all are worth bringing back. Bill has figured out which varieties grow best and are tastiest. He is not alone; across the country, hundreds of orchardists and farmers are also growing these old varieties, as well as heirloom tomatoes, peaches, melons, and corn—to name just a few—so there's a good chance at least some type of heirloom is growing near you.

apple spread with lemon verbena

MAKES 3 CUPS

Serve this zesty spread with Pan-Fried Pork Loin Chops with Herbed Bread Crumbs (page 164). It is also great spooned over pancakes or rolled in crêpes.

1 tablespoon vegetable oil

1 shallot, minced

Kosher salt

6 firm, tart apples, such as Newtown Pippin, Mutsu or Crispin, or Granny Smith, peeled, cored, and diced

2 large sprigs fresh lemon verbena or thyme

2 tablespoons sugar

¼ cup white wine, such as Chardonnay, Riesling, or Gewürztraminer

2 tablespoons champagne vinegar

HEAT THE OIL in a large saucepan over medium-low heat. Add the shallot with a pinch of salt and cook, stirring occasionally, until soft and golden, about 6 minutes.

Add the apples and 1 sprig of the lemon verbena, cut in pieces if it is too big for the pot. Stir to coat the apples with the shallot. Stir in the sugar and cook over medium heat until the apples begin to soften, adding a little water if the pan gets too dry, 6 to 8 minutes. Add the wine and vinegar. Turn the heat to medium-high and cook, stirring frequently to prevent sticking, until the liquid is evaporated and the apples are soft and spreadable but still have some shape, about 20 minutes. Remove and discard the lemon verbena sprig.

Strip the leaves from the remaining sprig of lemon verbena. Chop the leaves finely and stir them into the apple mixture. Season to taste with salt. Let cool completely before serving. The pâté can be refrigerated for up to 1 week.

beet and cranberry chutney

MAKES 5 CUPS

Serve this vibrant sweet and sour condiment with roasted or grilled pork or at Thanksgiving dinner in place of the usual cranberry relish.

3 oranges

¼ cup vegetable oil

1 large onion, finely diced

Kosher salt

1 (2-inch) piece fresh ginger, peeled and grated

1½ pounds red or Chioggia beets, peeled and finely chopped

Freshly ground black pepper

2 cups fresh cranberries

5 whole cloves

1 cinnamon stick

½ cup red wine vinegar

½ cup packed light brown sugar

USING A vegetable peeler, remove the zest from 1 of the oranges and set aside. Squeeze the juice from all 3 oranges and set aside.

In a Dutch oven or other heavy-bottomed pot, heat the oil over low heat and add the onion with a pinch of salt. Cook, stirring occasionally to avoid browning, until soft and translucent, about 10 minutes. Add the ginger and cook, stirring, for 2 minutes. Add the beets, season with salt and pepper, and stir to coat the beets with the oil. Add the orange zest, cranberries, cloves, and cinnamon stick. Stir and cook for another 5 minutes as the flavors begin to meld.

Add the orange juice, raise the heat to medium-high, and bring to a boil. Reduce the heat and simmer until the beets are tender and starting to break down, about 1½ hours. Add a little water if the mixture begins to look too dry. Add the vinegar and sugar and simmer to reduce to a thick consistency, 10 to 15 minutes. Taste for seasoning and adjust as needed with salt and pepper. The chutney can be used immediately or refrigerated for up to 2 weeks; the flavors will improve as the chutney sits.

preserved lemons

MAKES 12 LEMONS

12 Meyer or other lemons, plus
    more for juicing
¾ cup kosher salt
Fresh lemon juice, as needed

Any type of lemon can be preserved this way, although Meyer lemons are particularly good candidates because of their excellent flavor and soft, thin skins.

To use preserved lemons, remove one from the jar and slice it lengthwise into quarters. Scrape off the pulp and white pith and mince the skin. In some recipes the pulp is added as well as the chopped rind. The sharp salt and citrus flavor of preserved lemons is welcome in a wide variety of dishes. They are delicious in Albacore Tuna with Preserved Lemon and Olive Relish (page 120), or stir the minced rind into slow-simmered stew, or even into tuna, chicken, or bean salads.

WASH FOUR 1-pint glass canning jars, their rings, and lids in a dishwasher or with hot, soapy water and rinse them thoroughly. Place the jars in the canner (or in a large pot fitted with a metal rack) and cover with hot water. Bring the water to a boil and boil vigorously for 10 minutes. You may leave the jars in the hot water while you prepare the lemons.

Scrub the lemons well under cold running water and dry them with a towel. Holding a lemon over a bowl to catch any juices, use a paring knife to cut 4 evenly spaced slits lengthwise down the lemon, leaving the ends attached. The lemons should be left whole, so be careful not to cut so deep that they separate into sections. Repeat with all of the lemons.

Drain the jars. Generously pack the slits with the salt and layer the lemons in the jars, sprinkling salt between each layer. Push the lemons down firmly to pack as many as possible into each jar and so they release their juice. Top the jar with a final layer of salt and pour over any of the collected juices.

Tightly cover the jars and let sit at room temperature for 2 days. The jars will contain some juice after this period. Pour in enough freshly squeezed lemon juice to cover the lemons. Depending on how juicy the lemons are, you may need just a little or quite a bit of fresh lemon juice to cover the lemons. Estimate how much juice you'll need to fill each one. In general, 1 lemon yields 3 tablespoons lemon juice.

Place the jars in the refrigerator until the peels are soft and ready to eat, about 2 weeks. The lemons will keep for up to 1 year stored in the refrigerator.

lemon mayonnaise

3 large egg yolks

Kosher salt

1½ cups extra-virgin olive oil

Grated zest and juice of 1 small
lemon

Freshly ground black pepper

OPTIONAL FLAVORINGS

1 to 2 tablespoons chopped drained
capers

1 tablespoon chopped anchovies

1 to 2 tablespoons chopped fresh
flat-leaf parsley, chervil, or
chives

1 to 2 teaspoons chopped fresh
thyme, oregano, or marjoram

1 large clove garlic, minced or
pounded to a paste in a mortar

MAKES ABOUT 1²/₃ CUPS

Mayonnaise is easy to make at home, and the flavor of homemade mayonnaise is far superior to that of store-bought. If you're in a rush, you can make mayonnaise in the food processor, but the texture is much nicer when made by hand. The oil used has an enormous effect on the result, so taste your olive oil before using it to make the mayonnaise. Use a stronger olive oil if you prefer its strong taste, but if you prefer a milder flavor, use a fruitier, mellower oil. This recipe has a pronounced lemony flavor; if you prefer a more subtle lemon flavor, omit the zest; or change the accent of the mayonnaise with any of the additions listed at left.

IN A MEDIUM BOWL set on a damp towel to keep it steady, whisk the egg yolks with a pinch of salt. Whisking constantly, add the oil a few drops at a time until the mixture begins to thicken and emulsify. Then add the oil in a slow, steady stream, whisking quickly the whole time, until the mayonnaise is thick and glossy.

If the mayonnaise loses its emulsion, or breaks, while you are whisking in the oil, the problem can be fixed: Crack another egg yolk in a clean bowl and slowly whisk in the broken mixture. Whisk in the rest of the oil until the mayonnaise reaches the right consistency.

Whisk in the lemon juice, zest, and any other desired flavoring. Adjust the seasoning with salt and pepper. Use immediately, or cover and refrigerate for up to 2 days.

vegetable stock

2 yellow onions, quartered

2 carrots, cut into 2-inch pieces

4 ribs celery, cut into 2-inch pieces

3 pounds total other vegetables, such as asparagus ends, pea pods, mushroom stems, fennel fronds, leek greens, or green garlic tops or additional onion, carrots, and celery

6 sprigs fresh parsley

4 sprigs fresh thyme

2 fresh or dried bay leaves

COMBINE THE ONIONS, carrots, celery, other vegetables, parsley, thyme, and bay leaves in a large stockpot and add 3 quarts cold water. Bring to a boil, skimming off any impurities as they rise to the top. Reduce the heat and simmer for about 1 hour, or until the stock has a lovely vegetable flavor.

Strain the stock through a fine mesh strainer, discarding the solids, and cool to room temperature. Cover and refrigerate for up to 3 days or freeze for up to 6 months.

chicken stock

5 pounds chicken bones: necks,
  backs, leg bones, and/or whole
  carcasses
2 yellow onions, quartered
2 small carrots, cut into 2-inch
  pieces
2 ribs celery, cut into 2-inch pieces
2 fresh dried bay leaves

PUT THE CHICKEN bones in a large stockpot and add 4 quarts cold water. Bring to a boil over high heat, skimming off any impurities as they rise to the top. Just as the water comes to a boil, add the onions, carrots, celery, and bay leaves. Reduce the heat and simmer gently for about 4 hours or until the stock has a nice, rich flavor.

Turn off the heat and let the simmering subside. Pour the stock though a fine mesh strainer, discarding the solids. Cool the stock to room temperature and then cover and refrigerate. Remove any solidified fat from the top before using. The stock will keep refrigerated for up to 3 days or can be frozen for up to 6 months.

fish stock

MAKES ABOUT 1½ QUARTS

¼ cup white wine

1½ to 2 pounds fish bones, heads,
  and fins

1 yellow onion, sliced

1 carrot, sliced

1 rib celery, sliced

4 sprigs fresh thyme

2 fresh or dried bay leaves

POUR THE white wine into a stockpot and add the fish bones on top. Place the pot over medium-high heat and bring to a simmer (you will see steam though the fish bones). Cook for 30 seconds and then add the onion, carrot, celery, thyme, and bay leaves. Add 6 cups cold water.

Bring the water to a boil, skimming off any impurities as they rise to the top. Reduce the heat and simmer gently for about 30 minutes. The stock should have a fresh fish flavor. Strain though a fine mesh strainer, discarding the solids, and cool to room temperature. Cover and refrigerate for up to 2 days or freeze for up to 4 months.

pork stock

4 pounds pork bones

2 yellow onions, quartered

1 carrot, cut into 2-inch pieces

2 ribs celery, cut into 2-inch pieces

2 fried or dried bay leaves

4 whole black peppercorns

HEAT THE OVEN to 475°F.

Arrange the pork bones in a single layer in a roasting pan or baking sheet with steep sides. Divide them between 2 pans if necessary. Roast in the oven until evenly browned, turning halfway through, about 30 minutes.

Transfer the bones to a stockpot and place the hot roasting pan over medium heat. Pour in ½ cup water and scrape up any meaty bits. Pour the liquid into the stockpot. Add 4 quarts cold water and bring to a boil, skimming away any impurities that rise to the top. When the water boils, add the onions, carrot, celery, bay leaves, and peppercorns. Reduce the heat and simmer for 5 hours or until the stock has a rich pork flavor.

Strain the stock, discarding the solids, and cool to room temperature. Cover and refrigerate. Remove any solidified fat from the top before using. The stock will keep refrigerated for up to 3 days or can be frozen for up to 6 months.

beef stock

MAKES ABOUT 2½ QUARTS

5 pounds beef bones

½ cup red wine

2 yellow onions, quartered

2 small carrots, cut into 2-inch
  pieces

2 ribs celery, cut into 2-inch pieces

6 whole black peppercorns

2 fresh or dried bay leaves

HEAT THE OVEN to 475°F.

Arrange the bones in a single layer in a large roasting pan or baking sheet with steep sides; use 2 pans if necessary. Roast in the oven until evenly browned, 30 to 45 minutes, turning the bones once.

Transfer the bones to a large stockpot. Pour the red wine into the hot roasting pan and place the pan over medium heat, scraping the bottom to dislodge any meaty bits. Pour the wine into the stockpot with the bones. Add 4 quarts cold water and bring to a boil, skimming off any impurities as they rise to the top. When the water is just boiling, add the onions, carrots, celery, peppercorns, and bay leaves. Reduce the heat and simmer gently for about 5 hours or until the stock has a rich beef flavor.

Strain the stock, discarding the solids, and cool to room temperature. Cover and refrigerate. Remove any solidified fat from the top before using. The stock will keep refrigerated for up to 3 days or can be frozen for up to 6 months.

desserts

ZABAGLIONE WITH MUSCAT ICE WINE

———

BLUEBERRY GRANITA

———

FRESH STRAWBERRY BAVARIAN

———

QUINCE COOKED IN RED WINE WITH AGED SHEEP'S CHEESE AND HAZELNUTS

———

PAVLOVA WITH HACHIYA PERSIMMONS

———

PEACHES SOAKED IN GRAPPA WITH GOAT CHEESE AND CHESTNUT HONEY

———

CHAMOMILE-POACHED PEARS WITH LATE-HARVEST RIESLING CRÈME ANGLAISE

AND KUMQUATS

———

FRIED SWEET RICOTTA

———

MIXED BERRY TART WITH MEYER LEMON PASTRY CREAM

———

RHUBARB COBBLER

———

UPSIDE-DOWN FRESH FIG CAKE

———

ORANGE AND ALMOND CAKE

———

DARK CHOCOLATE AND LAVENDER TRUFFLES

———

CHOCOLATE ROSEMARY CAKE

———

FRESH FRUIT COULIS

———

GRAPE AND WALNUT SCHIACCIATA

zabaglione with muscat ice wine

SERVES 4

4 large egg yolks

¼ cup sugar

Pinch of kosher salt

⅓ cup muscat or other fruity, sweet wine

Fresh fruit for serving

California winemaker Randall Grahm of Bonny Doon vineyards has participated in more of our dinners than any other winemaker. In fact, his participation with our organization—and this version of zabaglione—goes back to the Farmer Dinners we used to hold at Gabriella Café, back in the days when we brought the farmers to the restaurant instead of taking the restaurant to the farmers. Zabaglione is a centuries-old dessert, traditionally made with sweet Marsala, which I replaced with Bonny Doon's Vin de Glacière Muscat on the night Randall came to Gabriella Café. Ice wines are made either by leaving the grapes on the vines so late in the season that they literally freeze on the vine or through mechanical means; the grapes are pressed while still frozen. The resulting wine, which is sweet yet high in acidity, works well in this foamy dessert with fruits that are not highly acidic, such as fresh berries or peaches.

BRING A POT with 2 inches of water in it to a simmer.

In a stainless-steel bowl that fits over the pot without touching the water, combine the egg yolks, sugar, and salt. Whisk by hand or with a hand-held electric mixer until the eggs are pale and light, about 3 minutes. Whisking constantly, slowly add the wine.

Place the bowl over the pot of simmering water and continue to whisk constantly until the mixture is thick and doubled in volume, 8 to 10 minutes. It is important that the mixture doesn't get too hot, or it will curdle. If you notice it is heating too fast, remove the bowl from the pot and continue whisking off the heat until it cools. Return the bowl to the heat and continue whisking until the zabaglione just holds its shape when you pull up the whisk and it's foamy.

Spoon the fruit into dessert bowls and top with the warm zabaglione.

blueberry granita

SERVES 4 TO 6

3½ cups fresh blueberries
½ cup superfine sugar
1 teaspoon grated lemon zest
1 tablespoon fresh lemon juice
Crème fraîche or unsweetened
    whipped cream, for serving

The pure flavor of blueberries, with its subtle undertones of warm spices, is the focus here, so it's perfect for the height of blueberry season, when the bushes are bursting with plump, dark berries and the farmers' markets are brimming with baskets of the fruit. Granita may be made up to two days in advance and kept in a covered container in the freezer; scrape the granita with a fork to fluff and lighten it just before serving. SEE PHOTOGRAPH ON PAGE 212.

COMBINE 2½ cups of the blueberries and the sugar in a food processor and blend until very smooth. Strain the puree though a fine mesh strainer, using a wooden spoon to help press out all the juice. Discard any remaining solids.

Add ¾ cup water, the lemon zest, and juice to the blueberry purée. Pour the mixture into a shallow nonreactive pie plate, baking dish, or tray. Place the dish in the freezer and stir every hour with a fork, crushing and scraping as the ice forms. When the mixture is evenly frozen and icy, after about 4 hours, scrape once again to fluff and lighten the crystals.

Spoon the granita into chilled glasses and top with the remaining 1 cup fresh blueberries and a dollop of crème fraîche. Serve immediately.

fresh strawberry bavarian

SERVES 8

A classic Bavarian cream is based on an egg custard, but eggless, gelatin-thickened mousse is often called a Bavarian when it is unmolded, as it is here. No matter what you call it, and molded in anything from an elegant fluted mold to a simple rounded bowl, this dessert is an elegant showcase for delicious, ripe strawberries.

1 tablespoon unflavored gelatin

2 to 3 pints fresh strawberries, hulled, plus more for garnish, if desired

⅔ cups superfine sugar

2 tablespoons fresh lemon juice

1 cup heavy cream

½ teaspoon vanilla extract

PLACE A 5-cup mold or eight 8-ounce molds or ramekins in the refrigerator to chill.

Pour 3 tablespoons cold water into a small saucepan and sprinkle the gelatin on top. Set aside for 10 minutes to soften.

In a food processor, purée enough of the strawberries to make 2 cups purée. Transfer the purée to a large bowl. Add the sugar and lemon juice and stir until the sugar is dissolved.

Using an electric mixer or a whisk, beat the cream with the vanilla until it holds stiff peaks. Set aside in the refrigerator.

Heat the gelatin and water over low heat, stirring until the gelatin is completely dissolved.

Set the bowl with the strawberry mixture in a bowl of ice and water. Quickly whisk the gelatin mixture into the strawberry mixture; continue whisking until the mixture thickens to the consistency of raw egg whites, about 10 minutes. Remove the bowl from the ice and fold in the whipped cream, working quickly.

Remove the mold from the refrigerator. Wet the inside of the mold with cold water and shake out the excess, or very lightly oil the inside of the mold. Pour in the Bavarian mixture. Refrigerate for 8 hours or overnight.

When ready to serve, slice fresh strawberries for garnish, if desired. Dip the bottom of the mold in warm water for 5 seconds for thin molds and 10 seconds for thicker or glass or ceramic molds. Place a plate over the top of the mold and flip over the mold to invert the Bavarian onto the plate. If the Bavarian does not unmold easily, gently slip the tip of a thin knife into the side of the inverted mold to release the vacuum. Top with the fresh sliced berries and serve immediately.

quince cooked in red wine with aged sheep's-milk cheese and hazelnuts

SERVES 4 TO 6

This makes an excellent dessert course or can start a meal when accompanied by lightly dressed peppery greens, such as watercress or peppercress, arugula, or radicchio. Sheep's-milk cheeses (page 224) are delicious; I'm pleased to see them growing in popularity.

⅓ cup hazelnuts

2 cups red wine

2 tablespoons sugar

½ teaspoon kosher salt

10 black peppercorns

4 sprigs fresh thyme

4 large quince

1 (6- to 8-ounce) wedge of aged sheep's-milk cheese

HEAT THE OVEN to 400°F.

Spread the hazelnuts on a baking sheet and toast them in the oven until they are fragrant and their skins begin to release, about 7 minutes. Cool briefly and then rub the hazelnuts in a folded towel to remove the skins. Discard the skins and coarsely chop the hazelnuts. Set aside.

Combine the wine, 1 cup cold water, and the sugar, salt, peppercorns, and thyme in a large pot. Bring to a simmer. Meanwhile, peel the quince and cut them in half, removing the seeds and cores. Cut the halves into wedges about 1 inch thick.

Add the quince to the red wine mixture and place a sheet of parchment paper cut to fit the pan directly on the surface of the liquid. Simmer gently until a paring knife slides easily into the quince with no resistance, 20 to 40 minutes. The quince will not necessarily all become tender at the same time, so remove the wedges as they are ready with a slotted spoon and let cool on a plate.

Strain off up to 1 cup of the cooking liquid and pour it into a small saucepan. Cook over medium-high heat until reduced to a thin syrup that will coat the back of a spoon but can still be easily drizzled, about 10 minutes.

Arrange the quince wedges on 4 to 6 salad plates. Break off small chunks of cheese with your fingers or shave off long pieces using a vegetable peeler and sprinkle over the quince. Drizzle with some of the reduced wine syrup, top with the chopped hazelnuts, and serve.

pavlova with hachiya persimmons

SERVES 6 TO 8

4 large egg whites

Pinch of kosher salt

¾ cup superfine sugar

1 teaspoon cornstarch, plus extra
for dusting the baking sheet

1 teaspoon white wine vinegar

½ teaspoon vanilla extract

3 very ripe Hachiya persimmons

1 cup heavy cream

The pavlova originated in New Zealand, but we have been making a variation of this meringue in the United States for years. In New Zealand, the dessert is often served at Christmas, a summer holiday because the country is in the southern hemisphere, so it is typically served with strawberries or other mixed berries. I, too, like to serve this around Christmas, but because Christmas falls during our winter, I use persimmons. The meringue has a crisp exterior and a soft interior. Hachiya persimmons are more oblong than the rounder Fuyu persimmons. They should not be eaten until they are very ripe, as unripe Hachiyas are extremely astringent.

HEAT THE OVEN to 225°F.

Using an electric mixer on medium-low speed, beat the egg whites with the salt until they become frothy. Gradually increase the speed to medium-high. Beat until the whites form soft peaks when the beater is lifted out of them. Add the sugar gradually, beating constantly. When all of the sugar is added, continue beating on high speed until the mixture is glossy and stiff enough to cut with a knife, about 5 minutes. Add the cornstarch, vinegar, and vanilla and beat for 30 seconds to incorporate.

Meanwhile, line a large baking sheet with parchment paper and dust it with cornstarch. Mound the meringue mixture in the center of the tray and form it into a 7-inch round; it will be about 3 inches tall. Form a dent in the center. The meringue will not rise or change shape at all during baking.

Bake until the pavlova begins to turn golden and it is firm to the touch, about 1½ hours. Check the pavlova from time to time (starting after the first 30 minutes of cooking if you must open the oven door to check), and if it is browning too much, turn the oven down 10 to 15 degrees. Turn off the oven and let the pavlova cool inside, undisturbed. You may bake the pavlova the night before you plan to serve it and leave it to cool overnight in the oven.

Cut the persimmons in half and scoop the flesh into a bowl. Mash any firm membrane with a fork or a hand blender. In a separate bowl, whip the cream to soft peaks.

Place the pavlova on a serving platter and spoon the whipped cream into the center. Spoon the persimmon pulp over the cream. Slice and serve.

peaches soaked in grappa with goat cheese and chestnut honey

SERVES 6

Sweet, ripe peaches are like little sponges for strong grappa, creating one of the flavor contrasts that make this dish so heavenly. Served with tangy goat cheese and not-too-sweet, rich chestnut honey, this is a divine dessert. There's no need to discard whatever grappa is left after the peaches have macerated; the peaches leave behind excellent aroma and flavor as well as a bit of sweetness. Strain it and drink it as an after-dinner drink, just as you would any grappa.

3 ripe peaches

1 cup good-quality reserve grappa

6 tablespoons fresh goat cheese (about 4 ounces), at room temperature

About 2 tablespoons chestnut honey

BRING A SAUCEPAN of water to a boil and prepare a bowl of ice water. Cut a small X in the base of each peach. Put the peaces in the boiling water for 30 seconds to release the skin. Remove them from the water with a slotted spoon and plunge them into the ice water to cool. Peel the skin off each peach and cut them in half from the top to the base. Carefully pry each peach apart and discard the pit. Place the peach halves in a dish just large enough to hold them all in a single layer. Pour the grappa on top and gently turn the peaches to coat them well. Set aside at room temperature to macerate for at least 2 hours, periodically turning the peaches.

Arrange the peaches on a serving platter. Put 1 tablespoon goat cheese in the center of each one and drizzle with the chestnut honey before serving.

chamomile-poached pears with late-harvest riesling crème anglaise and kumquats

SERVES 6

For this elegant autumn dessert, both the pears and the crème anglaise can be made in advance and then put together just before serving, so it is a great dish for company. Late-harvest Riesling is sweet without being cloying and has herbaceous and fruity qualities, which makes a good match for pears poached in chamomile flowers. The colorful kumquat "coins" add beauty and a welcome bit of sourness.

½ cup whole milk

½ cup heavy cream

2 large egg yolks

1¾ cups sugar

4 teaspoons late-harvest Riesling or other sweet wine or sherry

3 pears, preferably Bosc

1 tablespoon fresh or dried chamomile flowers or

1 chamomile tea bag

10 kumquats, for serving

IN A MEDIUM saucepan over medium heat, bring the milk and cream just to a simmer. Remove the pan from the heat.

In a medium bowl, whisk the eggs yolks and ¼ cup of the sugar vigorously until lightened in color. Whisking constantly, slowly add the hot milk mixture in a steady stream. Transfer the mixture to the saucepan and cook over medium-low heat, stirring constantly with a wooden spoon, until it is thickened and registers around 175°F on an instant-read thermometer. The custard should coat the back of a spoon and leave a trail when you draw your finger across it.

Remove the pan from the heat and stir in the Riesling. Pour the mixture through a fine mesh strainer into a bowl and place the bowl in a larger bowl of ice water. Stir the custard sauce until it is cool. Cover and refrigerate until ready to use or for up to 2 days.

Peel the pears and cut them in half lengthwise, leaving the stem attached to one half. Using a small paring knife, remove the seeds and the base core.

Have ready a medium saucepan big enough to fit the pears. Cut a piece of parchment paper to the size of the pan. Combine the remaining 1½ cups sugar and 3 cups cold water in the saucepan. Bring to a gentle simmer over medium-low heat and stir with a wooden spoon until all the sugar is melted. Wrap the chamomile flowers in a piece of cheesecloth or place them into a tea ball and add them, or the tea bag, if using, to the syrup. Simmer gently for 2 minutes. Add the pears and cover with the parchment paper. Simmer gently until the pears are tender when pierced with a thin knife, 15 to 25 minutes, depending on their firmness. The pears on the bottom may need to be rotated to the top as they simmer so they cook evenly. Remove the pears as they are done with a slotted spoon and set on a plate to cool.

Remove and discard the chamomile and cool the syrup separately. Return the cooled pears to the cooled syrup and until ready to use or refrigerate for up to 1 day.

Cut the kumquats into thin coins, removing any seeds.

When ready to serve, gently reheat the pears in their poaching syrup. Place 1 pear half in each of 6 dessert bowls with a small bit of syrup. Spoon the crème anglaise over the pears, top with kumquat slices, and serve.

Old Chatham Sheepherding Company, Old Chatham, New York

Tom and Nancy Clark started Old Chatham Sheepherding Company in 1993 with 150 sheep. Today, this sheep dairy in New York's Hudson River Valley has grown to more than 1,000 sheep whose milk is used to make hand-crafted cheese, ricotta, and yogurt used by chefs all across America. We teamed up there for a dinner in early autumn with Chef Bryce Whittlesey of the elegant Wheatleigh Inn in Lenox, Massachusetts, to support Berkshire Grown (www.berkshiregrown.org). With its red barn and rolling hills, Old Chatham is a classic Northeastern affair, and we were there when the weather was just turning crisp and the leaves turning color. The setting was already magical, and the phenomenally good cheese made it all the more so.

Sheep's-milk cheese and ricotta are far more complex and delicious than many cow's-milk cheeses. Cheesemakers in Europe have been using sheep's milk to make

some of the best cheeses in the world for centuries. Americans, however, have almost always preferred milder cow's-milk cheeses, going so far over the years as to reproduce feta and blue cheese using cow's milk in place of the traditional sheep's or goat's milk. Demand for sheep's-milk cheese is rising, however, and I am not the only person who credits Tom and Nancy with playing a large part in this shift.

Sheep's-milk cheese has a tang and sharpness that enlivens both sweet and savory dishes; it's as good with spicy salumi as with a plate of fresh fruit. Look for Old Chatham products locally or online (www.blacksheepcheese.com).

fried sweet ricotta

2 cups whole sheep's- or cow's-milk
    ricotta

2 large eggs, beaten

¼ cup sugar

Grated or minced zest of 1 small
    lemon, minced

Vegetable oil, for frying

¼ cup all-purpose flour, or as
    needed, plus more for dusting

Powdered sugar, for serving

These sweet little puffs with a hint of citrus usually disappear as quickly as we can fry them. I try to use as little flour as possible to allow the flavors of the tangy ricotta and lemon to come through cleanly, but this is not always possible, since ricotta can be quite wet even after draining. Add just as much flour as you need to make the batter firm enough that you can gently roll balls of it in flour and transfer them to the oil without having them fall apart. You may need to experiment a bit, so add the flour a small amount at a time and try to form a ball after each addition; you can always add more flour as needed. To serve, pile the fritters on a platter so people can simply grab them, or plate individual servings and spoon a fruit coulis (page 241) around them.

SPOON THE ricotta into the center of a large piece of doubled cheesecloth and tie the ends together tightly with butcher's twine. Tie the bundle to the handle of a wooden spoon and lay the spoon across the top of a bowl deep enough that the ricotta bundle does not touch the bottom. Refrigerate overnight. Squeeze the ricotta bundle firmly the next morning to force out all the liquid. The ricotta should be very dry; if you form a tablespoonful into a ball, it should hold its shape.

In a large bowl, combine the ricotta, eggs, sugar, and lemon zest. Add the flour 1 tablespoon at a time until the mixture holds its shape.

Pour the oil into a large, deep pot, such as a Dutch oven, so it is at least 2½ inches deep but comes no more than halfway up the sides of the pot. Attach a candy or deep frying thermometer to the side of the pot and heat the oil over medium heat to 365°F.

Scoop out 1 tablespoon of the ricotta mixture and form into balls. With floured hands, roll each ball in flour, dusting off any excess. Drop a few balls at a time into the hot oil and fry until golden brown, about 1 minute. Use a mesh skimmer or slotted spoon to remove the fried ricotta from the oil and drain on paper towels.

Arrange the fried ricotta on a serving platter and dust with powdered sugar. Serve hot.

mixed berry tart with meyer lemon pastry cream

MAKES ONE 9-INCH TART; SERVES 6 TO 8

The Meyer lemon, commonly believed to be a cross between a lemon and an orange or a mandarin, is slightly sweet without the tartness of a regular lemon and very juicy. Here it adds complexity and fragrance to both the pastry cream and the berries, which are macerated in its juice. For this stunning dessert, use whatever mix of berries looks good at the market.

1 Meyer lemon

½ cup plus 1 tablespoon sugar

2 tablespoons unbleached all-purpose flour

⅛ teaspoon kosher salt

2 large eggs

1 large egg yolk

1½ cups whole milk

1½ pints mixed fresh berries, such as blueberries, raspberries, and blackberries

Tart Shell (recipe follows), cooled

REMOVE THE ZEST from the lemon with a vegetable peeler and chop it finely. Set the chopped zest aside. Squeeze 1 tablespoon of the juice from the lemon and set the juice aside.

In a medium bowl, whisk together ½ cup of the sugar, the flour, and the salt. Gradually whisk in the eggs and the egg yolk until smooth. Bring the milk to a boil in a heavy-bottomed saucepan. Whisking constantly, slowly pour about one-third of the milk into the egg mixture. Whisking constantly, pour the entire egg mixture back into the remaining milk in the pan. Whisk in the lemon zest. Place the pan over medium heat and cook, whisking constantly, making sure to scrape the bottom and corners of the pan, until the mixture thickens and comes to a boil. Boil, still whisking, for 1 minute. Remove from the heat and pour the pastry cream into a bowl. Press a piece of plastic wrap flush to the surface to prevent a skin from forming. Refrigerate until cold, about 4 hours, or overnight.

Mix the berries with the remaining 1 tablespoon sugar and the reserved lemon juice. Toss together and let sit for about 10 minutes to macerate.

To assemble the tart, remove the shell from the pan and place it on a serving plate. Spoon the pastry cream into the shell and smooth the top. Pour the berries and their juices on top and serve.

tart shell

1⅓ cups unbleached all-purpose
flour
1 tablespoon sugar
¼ teaspoon kosher salt
8 tablespoons (1 stick) unsalted
butter, cut into pieces and chilled
2 large egg yolks
3 tablespoons ice water

MAKES ONE 9-INCH PREBAKED TART SHELL

PULSE THE FLOUR, sugar, and salt in a food processor until combined. Sprinkle the butter on top and pulse until the mixture resembles coarse bread crumbs. Add 1 of the yolks and 1 tablespoon of the water and pulse until the dough just comes together, adding the remaining water 1 tablespoon at a time, if necessary. Press the dough into a disk, wrap it tightly in plastic, and refrigerate it for at least 1 hour or overnight.

Remove the tart dough from the refrigerator and let stand for a few minutes if it is not malleable enough to roll. Between sheets of plastic wrap, overlapping if they are not wide enough, or on a lightly floured surface, roll the tart dough ⅛ inch thick. Fit it into a 9-inch tart pan with a removable bottom, trimming the edges. Refrigerate for at least 30 minutes.

Heat the oven to 425°F.

Line the pan with parchment paper and pour in dried beans or pie weights, pushing them up against the sides of the pan. Bake for 20 minutes. Remove the parchment and weights and prick the bottom and sides with a fork. Bake for an additional 5 to 7 minutes until the tart shell is golden brown; check halfway through baking and prick any bubbles with a fork.

Meanwhile, mix the remaining egg yolk with a pinch of salt. Brush the surface of the tart crust with the egg yolk mixture, and then bake for 1 to 2 minutes, until the yolk is set. Remove the tart shell from the oven and let cool completely.

rhubarb cobbler

SERVES 6 TO 8

3 pounds rhubarb

1½ cups sugar

1 tablespoon grated orange zest

¾ cup buttermilk

4 tablespoons (½ stick) unsalted butter, melted and cooled

1 large egg, at room temperature

1½ cups unbleached all-purpose flour

1½ teaspoons baking powder

¼ teaspoon kosher salt

Whipped Cream (recipe follows), Brown Sugar Crème Fraîche (page 234), or vanilla ice cream, for serving

Many recipes for baked fruit desserts call for mixing flour, cornstarch, or tapioca with the fruit to thicken the juices during baking and prevent sogginess. I prefer to avoid these thickeners because I find they mask the bright flavors of fresh fruit. But those juices do need to be dealt with, and this recipe does that by first cooking the rhubarb on the stovetop and then reducing the extracted juice. This method not only reduces excess liquid, it actually concentrates the rhubarb's flavor.

TRIM THE RHUBARB and cut crosswise on an angle into 1-inch pieces. Place the rhubarb in a medium saucepan with 1¼ cups of the sugar and the orange zest. Cook over low heat, stirring occasionally, until the rhubarb is softened and has released its liquid, about 20 minutes.

Position a rack in the bottom third of the oven. Place a foil-lined baking sheet underneath the oven rack that will hold the cobbler. Heat the oven to 375°F.

Using a slotted spoon, transfer the rhubarb to a 2-quart baking dish with 2-inch-high sides, or eight 10- to 12-ounce ramekins for individual cobblers. If using individual ramekins, arrange them on a baking sheet. Simmer the liquid remaining in the saucepan over medium heat until it is reduced by half and is thick and syrupy, about 10 minutes. Pour it over the rhubarb.

In a medium bowl, whisk together the buttermilk, butter, and egg. In another bowl, whisk together the remaining ¼ cup sugar with the flour, baking powder, and salt. Add the dry ingredients to the wet ingredients and slowly stir just until incorporated. Do not overmix.

Spoon the batter over the rhubarb, covering the surface. Bake until golden brown and bubbling and a skewer inserted into the topping comes out clean, 45 to 50 minutes for a large cobbler, 20 to 25 minutes for individual cobblers.

Let rest for 10 minutes and serve warm with the whipped cream.

whipped cream

1 cup heavy cream
Up to 2 tablespoons sugar (optional)
1 teaspoon vanilla extract (optional)

MAKES 2 CUPS

It is helpful, especially if the weather is warm, to place the bowl and beaters in the freezer for 30 minutes before whipping the cream.

PUT THE CREAM in a medium bowl and add the sugar and vanilla, if desired. Using a whisk or an electric mixer, whisk or beat at high speed until the cream holds soft peaks when the whisk or beater is lifted up and out of the bowl. The whipped cream is best used immediately, but it can be chilled for up to 1 hour before serving.

upside-down fresh fig cake

SERVES 8

This is a surprising twist on the classic pineapple upside-down cake and a delicious way to welcome summer figs. At other times of the year, you can use dried figs in place of the fresh, with excellent results; reconstitute them before using in warm water or red or white wine for 30 minutes.

12 tablespoons (1¼ sticks) unsalted butter

½ cup packed light brown sugar

2 tablespoons honey

10 fresh figs, stems removed, cut in half

1½ cups unbleached all-purpose flour

1½ teaspoons baking powder

¼ teaspoon kosher salt

¾ cup granulated sugar

1 teaspoon vanilla extract

2 large eggs

½ cup whole milk

HEAT THE OVEN to 350°F. Butter a 9-inch cake pan with 2-inch sides. Line the bottom of the pan with parchment paper and butter the parchment. In a small saucepan over medium-low heat or in the microwave oven, melt 4 tablespoons of the butter. Stir in the brown sugar and honey until smooth. Pour the sauce into the prepared cake pan. Arrange the figs, cut sides down, in concentric circles over the sauce. Set aside.

In a medium bowl, whisk together the flour, baking powder, and salt. In another bowl, using an electric mixer on medium speed, beat the remaining 8 tablespoons butter with the sugar and vanilla until lightened in color and texture, 2 to 3 minutes. Add the eggs 1 at a time, beating until well combined after each addition. Beating on low speed just until combined after each addition, add the dry ingredients in 3 parts, alternating with the milk in 2 parts, beginning and ending with the dry ingredients. Spoon the batter evenly over the figs.

Bake the cake until golden and a skewer inserted into center comes out clean, 45 to 55 minutes. Transfer the cake to a rack and cool in the pan for 50 minutes.

Run a thin knife around the sides of the pan to loosen. Place a serving platter on top of the pan and invert the cake. Gently lift off the pan and remove the parchment paper. Spoon over the cake any of the sauce that has run off and serve warm.

orange and almond cake

SERVES 8

2 medium thin-skinned oranges
(about 8 ounces each), washed

2 cups ground blanched or natural
almonds (about 8½ ounces)

6 large eggs yolks

6 large egg whites

1¼ cups sugar

Brown Sugar Crème Fraîche (recipe
follows), crème fraîche, or
unsweetened whipped cream
(page 229), for serving

Two whole oranges make this delicious flourless cake incredibly moist. Any variety of orange can be used, but those with thin skins, such as Valencia, are preferable; because you're eating the whole oranges, peels and all, try to use organic fruit. If you cannot find or prefer not to buy ground almonds, use an equal weight (8½ ounces, or about 1¾ cups) of whole blanched or natural almonds and carefully grind them in a food processor. To avoid overprocessing the nuts, pulse them in 1- or 2-second bursts until ground.

PUT THE ORANGES in a saucepan that fits both of them comfortably and has a tight-fitting lid. Fill the pan with water until the oranges are just covered. Bring to a boil and then simmer over low heat, covered, until the oranges are soft and can be easily pierced with a knife, about 2 hours. Check the pan from time to time and add more water if necessary; the oranges will not stay submerged, but they will cook all over if there is plenty of water in the pan. Remove the oranges from the water and set them aside to cool. (This step can be done up to 1 day ahead.)

Heat the oven to 375°F. Butter the bottom only of a 10-inch springform pan. Line the bottom with parchment or wax paper, and then butter the paper. Do not butter the sides of the pan.

Spread the ground almonds on a baking sheet and toast in the oven until fragrant and light golden brown, 5 to 7 minutes; watch carefully and shake the pan or stir the almonds occasionally to prevent them from burning. Transfer the nuts to a shallow bowl or plate to cool.

Reduce the oven temperature to 325°F.

Cut the oranges into wedges, removing any seeds. Put the oranges into the bowl of a food processor and process to a smooth paste, scraping down the sides of the bowl once or twice. Process the oranges in two batches if necessary. Set aside.

RECIPE CONTINUES

With an electric mixer, using the paddle attachment if possible, beat the egg yolks on medium-high speed until lightened in color and texture, about 1 minute. Gradually add the sugar. Beat on medium-high speed until the mixture is thick and pale, about 2 minutes. Fold in the almonds and then fold in the orange paste.

In a separate bowl, use a whisk or an electric mixer on medium-low speed to beat the egg whites until frothy. Gradually increase the speed to high. Beat until the whites form stiff peaks when the whisk or beater is lifted up out of them. Fold the egg whites into the orange mixture.

Pour the batter into the prepared pan and bake until the center is light brown, the edges are darker brown, and a skewer inserted in the center comes out clean, about 1 hour.

Transfer the pan to a rack and let the cake cool completely in the pan. Run a thin knife around the outside of the cake and remove the sides of the pan. If you wish to unmold the cake completely, invert it onto a plate or a rack and remove the parchment paper liner. Turn the cake right side up on a cake plate and serve with brown sugar crème fraîche.

brown sugar crème fraîche

MAKES 2½ CUPS

½ cup heavy cream
1½ tablespoons packed dark brown
   sugar
½ cup crème fraîche

With a light flavor of caramel and a welcome touch of sweetness, this topping is a nice accompaniment to a variety of desserts. It's particularly good with Rhubarb Cobbler (page 228) and Orange and Almond Cake (page 232).

IN A SMALL saucepan, combine the cream and brown sugar. Heat gently over low heat, stirring occasionally, until the sugar is completely melted. Remove the pan from the heat and let cool. Transfer the cream to a covered container and chill until cold.

When ready to serve, put the crème fraîche in a medium bowl. Whisking constantly or beating with a hand-held mixer, pour in the cream mixture. Continue to whisk or beat until the mixture holds soft peaks. Serve.

dark chocolate and lavender truffles

MAKES ABOUT 40 TRUFFLES

26 ounces dark chocolate

¾ cup heavy cream

6 fresh lavender flower sprigs or
2 teaspoons dried flower buds

2 tablespoons unsalted butter,
softened

1 cup superfine granulated sugar

Fragrant lavender is nice paired with earthy, slightly bitter dark chocolate, and these truffles are an elegant way to end the meal. The tempered chocolate coating is beautiful and functional, as it holds the tiny sugared lavender buds, which contribute yet more lavender flavor and look lovely. However, the process for tempering the chocolate and dipping the ganache balls can be time-consuming and tricky, so I sometimes forgo that entire process and simply roll the lavender-infused ganache balls in cocoa powder or powdered sugar. The result is a little less elegant but they are nonetheless delicious. Be sure the lavender you use is unsprayed and intended for consumption.

The main thing to look for when buying chocolate is the percentage of cocoa solids—that is, cocoa plus cocoa butter—the bar contains. I most often use chocolate with 60 to 70 percent cocoa solids. These chocolates are usually marked *bittersweet* or *semisweet,* but don't go by the labels alone; look for the percentage of cocoa solids, for some semisweet chocolates can have as little as 40 percent cocoa solids, which usually means more sweetness than chocolate flavor. I prefer to control the amount of sugar in a recipe myself. For these truffles in particular, I really want pure chocolate without a lot of extra sweetness so the lavender flavor can really come through. For me, this means 70 percent cocoa solids. Valrhona, Guittard, Lindt, and Scharffen Berger 70 percent dark chocolates are all good; the Scharffen Berger is the most bitter of the group. If you prefer a little more sweetness, try a chocolate with 60 to 65 percent cocoa solids.

Don't discard the lavender-infused syrup that is a wonderful byproduct of preparing the lavender garnish. It is great added to iced tea or mixed with fresh lemon juice and water or club soda for lavender lemonade.

CHOP THE CHOCOLATE into small pieces. Put 8 ounces of the chopped chocolate in a stainless-steel bowl and put 16 ounces in a second stainless-steel bowl. Set the remaining 2 ounces aside.

RECIPE CONTINUES

Combine the cream and 3 of the fresh lavender flowers or 1 teaspoon of the dried flowers in a small saucepan and heat just until it bubbles. Remove the pan from the heat and let stand to infuse, covered, for 5 minutes.

Return the cream to the heat and bring to a boil. Strain the hot cream mixture over the 8 ounces of chopped chocolate. Let sit for 30 seconds and then whisk gently to incorporate and make a smooth ganache. Strain in the remaining cream and mix well. The ganache should be smooth, not grainy. If there are still bits of unmelted chocolate in the mixture, place the bowl over a pot of hot—but not boiling—water and mix constantly until the remaining chocolate has melted. Be careful not to overheat the mixture or let any water get into the bowl of chocolate or you may break the emulsion. Let the mixture cool to room temperature.

Cut the butter into small pieces. When the chocolate mixture has cooled to warm room temperature, add a few pieces of butter at a time, stirring after each addition, until well incorporated. Cover the ganache with plastic wrap and put it in the refrigerator until firm, 15 to 30 minutes.

In a small saucepan, combine ½ cup of the sugar with ½ cup water. Heat over medium heat until the sugar is melted. Remove the individual buds from the remaining lavender flowers and stir them or the remaining 1 teaspoon dried lavender flowers into the sugar syrup. Simmer gently for about 5 minutes. Strain through a fine mesh strainer placed over a bowl (reserve the sugar syrup for another use) and dry the buds on a towel. Put the buds in the remaining sugar and stir to coat. Drop the coated lavender flowers into a fine mesh strainer and shake to sift away the excess sugar. Place the candied buds on a plate to dry and harden while you roll the truffles.

Line a large tray or rimmed baking sheet with parchment paper. Remove the bowl of ganache from the refrigerator. Roll small spoonfuls of the ganache into ¾- to 1-inch balls with your hands. When all of the ganache has been rolled, put the tray in the refrigerator while you temper the chocolate for coating.

Bring a saucepan filled with 2 inches water to a boil. Place the bowl of 16 ounces of chocolate over the hot water and melt slowly until the temperature of the chocolate reads 122°F to 125°F on a thermometer. Be careful not to overheat it and make sure no water gets into the bowl of chocolate or it will not harden properly later. Remove the bowl from the saucepan and cool the chocolate, gently stirring in the remaining 2 ounces chopped chocolate a small pinch at a time until the temperature reaches 85°F.

When the temperature reaches 85°F, place the bowl back over the saucepan of hot water and gently raise the temperature of the chocolate to between 87°F and 88°F. This should take 1 to 3 minutes. Check to see the chocolate has been properly tempered by placing a drop on a piece of parchment paper and refrigerating it. The drop should harden evenly and have a nice gloss.

Remove the ganache balls from the refrigerator. Using a fork (one with long, fine tines works best), dip the balls one by one into the tempered chocolate to coat. Hold the fork over the bowl briefly to allow any excess chocolate to drip off the truffle. Place the coated truffles back on the tray lined with parchment. Quickly place 2 or 3 of the candied lavender buds on top of each truffle, pressing down gently so they stick. Repeat with all of the remaining balls of ganache. Let the truffles harden at room temperature for about 1 hour.

If the tempered chocolate cools too much and begins to thicken, set the bowl over the saucepan of hot water, stirring occasionally, just until it returns to between 87°F and 88°F.

When the chocolate coating has set, remove the truffles from the sheet of parchment paper and gently trim off any excess chocolate at the base with a paring knife, if desired. The truffles will keep at room temperature for 2 weeks, stored in an airtight container.

chocolate rosemary cake

MAKES ONE 10-INCH CAKE; SERVES 14

12 ounces semisweet chocolate
 with 60% cocoa solids, chopped
1 cup plus 2 tablespoons
 (2¼ sticks) unsalted butter, cut
 into small pieces, plus more for
 greasing the pan
¾ cup heavy cream
3 rosemary sprigs
7 large eggs
¾ cup sugar
Whipped Cream (page 229), for
 serving

There are more versions of rich, flourless chocolate cake in the culinary world than anyone can possibly count. This one stands out among them because it is infused with the bold, earthy flavor of fresh rosemary. It's an unusual way to make good use of a late-summer abundance of rosemary in your herb garden. The quality of the chocolate you use will make a big difference in the final result, so use the best-quality dark semisweet chocolate you can find, with around 60 percent cocoa solids (see page 235).

HEAT THE OVEN to 350°F. Grease a 10-inch springform pan with butter and line the bottom with parchment or wax paper. Butter the paper and then dust the pan with flour, tapping out any excess. Set aside.

In a stainless-steel bowl placed over a saucepan of simmering water, heat the chocolate and butter, stirring occasionally, until melted and smooth.

In a small saucepan, combine the cream and rosemary. Heat until just starting to bubble and then remove from the heat. Cover and let stand to infuse for 7 minutes. Strain, discarding the rosemary, and set the cream aside.

In a large bowl, beat together the eggs and sugar until lightened in color. Whisking constantly, slowly add the melted chocolate mixture to the eggs. When fully incorporated, whisk in the cream thoroughly.

Pour the batter into the prepared pan. Bake just until the edges are set and the center is lightly set but jiggles slightly when the pan is gently nudged, 35 to 45 minutes.

Let the cake cool completely in the pan; it will fall and perhaps even crack a bit while cooling. When the cake is completely cool, run a paring knife along the sides of the pan to release it. Invert onto a rack or plate and remove the parchment paper. Turn right side up on a serving platter. Serve with whipped cream.

fresh fruit coulis

2 cups sliced strawberries, whole
blueberries, raspberries, or
blackberries, or diced mango,
peaches, or melon

3 tablespoons sugar, or to taste

2 teaspoons fresh lemon juice, or to
taste

This method can be used to make a bright, beautiful and flavorful sauce from almost any berry or soft, ripe fruit, such as peaches, mango, or melon. Fresh fruit sauces are delicious with a wide range of desserts. Use strawberries to make a sauce to accompany the Fresh Strawberry Bavarian (page 216), blueberries for a sauce to go with Blueberry Granita (page 215), or serve Fried Sweet Ricotta (page 225) with a sauce made from raspberries, mango, or any berry or other soft fruit. Straining the mixture is optional, but it's generally preferable to do so when using berries with lots of tiny seeds, such as raspberries, or fruit that can be fibrous, such as mango. Adjust the sugar and lemon juice to taste, depending on how sweet the fruit is.

COMBINE THE FRUIT, sugar, and lemon juice in a food processor or blender and process until smooth. Strain through a fine mesh sieve into a bowl, if desired. Taste and add more sugar or lemon juice as desired. Whisk in up to 1/4 cup water to thin the sauce if necessary. Serve at once or chill until ready to serve.

grape and walnut schiacciata

SERVES 6 TO 8

¾ cup warm water

1 package (about 2 teaspoons)
   active dry yeast

1 teaspoon plus 1 tablespoon sugar

⅓ cup extra-virgin olive oil, plus
   extra for brushing

2 cups unbleached all-purpose flour

½ teaspoon salt

2 cups stemmed small seedless
   black or red grapes (about
   1 pound)

½ cup chopped walnuts

Schiacciata, which means "squished" in Italian, is a general term used in Tuscany for any bread or cake that is flat and has been pressed down with one's fingers or a rolling pin. In other parts of Italy and here in the United States, we often see a similar product we call *focaccia.* This olive-oil–laced, faintly sweet flatbread is perfect in the fall, when tiny grapes are ripe. If your grapes are large or have tough skins, they'll also taste good when used here (actually it's an easy and tasty way to use up inferior grapes); but you'll have a trickier time getting them to stay put when kneading. Some recipes call for rolling the dough and then lining the grapes between layers, but I don't think this is necessary. This is an extremely forgiving flatbread, so don't worry too much about getting it just so; the grapes will soften into the bread during baking.

Schiacciata is great all by itself as dessert or laid out with a spread of olives and salumi for hors d'oeuvres. It's also delicious served alongside hard cheeses.

COMBINE THE WATER, yeast, and 1 teaspoon sugar in a measuring pitcher. Whisk briefly to combine and set aside for 5 to 10 minutes until foamy. Whisk in ⅓ cup of the olive oil.

Whisk the flour and salt together in a large bowl. Make a well in the center and gradually pour in the yeast mixture, using your hands or a fork to incorporate the flour little by little. When the dough begins to come together, add half of the grapes and mix with your hands to incorporate them into the dough. Turn the dough out onto the counter and knead it for 5 minutes until smooth, breaking the skins of some of the grapes as you knead. If the grapes roll out of the dough, let them go (but not too far); knead the dough without them and then work them in quickly at the end.

Alternatively, use an electric mixer with the dough hook attachment. After the flour and salt are whisked together, attach the bowl to the stand and, beating on low speed, gradually add in the yeast mixture. When the dough begins to come together, add half the grapes. Turn the mixer to medium-low speed and mix until smooth, about 2 minutes.

Form the dough into a ball and place it in a lightly oiled bowl. Brush the top with oil and cover with plastic wrap. Set aside until the dough has doubled in size, 1½ to 2 hours.

Brush a 13 x 9-inch baking sheet with at least ½-inch sides generously with olive oil. Press the dough into the prepared pan. If grapes fall out of the dough as you are pressing it into the pan, slip them under the flattened dough and twist the dough around them. Sprinkle the walnuts and any remaining grapes on top and press them into the flattened dough. Brush the top with olive oil and set aside to rise for an additional 30 minutes.

While the dough is rising, heat the oven to 425°F.

Sprinkle the remaining 1 tablespoon sugar over the top of the schiacchiata and bake for 20 minutes.

Reduce the oven temperature to 350° and bake the schiacciata for an additional 10 minutes, until golden brown. Let cool for about 5 minutes in the pan. Turn out onto a wooden board and serve warm or at room temperature, cut into slices.

menus

HERE'S a collection of menus accumulated over the years of Outstanding in the Field dinners. Our dinners are long affairs, beginning in the late afternoon and going until sundown, so we serve many courses. You may certainly cut a few courses from these proposed menus, and should in any case base your own menu on what's available locally. Visit your farmers' market to be inspired to create your own farm-to-table menu from what's being offered there.

Radishes with Anchovy Butter *(page 21)*
Fried Squash Blossoms Filled with Lavender Ricotta *(page 32)*
Salad of Santa Rosa Plums, Red Cabbage, Purslane, and Sunflower Petals *(page 51)*
Black Cod Wrapped in Fig Leaves with Grilled Summer Squash *(page 130)*
Upside-Down Fresh Fig Cake *(page 231)*

⊹⊱⋅⊰⊹

Goat Cheese Crostini with Sweet Pea Pesto *(page 22)*
Caramelized Carrot Salad *(page 46)*
Fresh Lamb Sausage and Lamb Kidneys *(pages 186 and 184)*
Stewed Fava Beans and Mint *(page 184)*
Green Garlic and Potato Gratin *(page 96)*
Mixed Berry Tart with Meyer Lemon Pastry Cream *(page 226)*

⊹⊱⋅⊰⊹

Savory Pecan, Parmesan, and Thyme Shortbread *(page 25)*
Chestnut Soup with Porcini Relish *(page 74)*
Roasted Pork with Fennel Seed and Herbs *(page 170)*
Rainbow Chard Tart *(page 92)*
Local Cheeses Served with Apple Spread with Lemon Verbena *(page 202)*
Grape and Walnut Schiacciata *(page 242)*

Tomato Water *(page 20)*

Corn Chowder with Marjoram *(page 60)*

Slashed Striped Bass Fillets with Herbs *(page 121)*

Deep-Fried Okra with a Buttermilk-Semolina Crust *(page 91)*

Haricot Vert and Early Girl Tomato Salad with Summer Savory *(page 48)*

Blueberry Granita *(page 215)*

⇢⊱·⊰⇠

Braised Broccoli Rabe and Cheese Bruschetta *(page 28)*

Butter Lettuce with Seared Chicken Livers and Radishes *(page 47)*

Chicken Saltimbocca *(page 150)*

Beet Greens with Lemon Juice and Extra-Virgin Olive Oil *(page 88)*

Potato, Sweet Chile, and Wild Fennel Salad *(page 56)*

Orange and Almond Cake *(page 232)*

⇢⊱·⊰⇠

Fresh Marinated Anchovies and Parsley Salad on Crostini *(page 29)*

Baby Turnip Soup *(page 68)*

Grass-Fed Beef Skirt Steak with Artichoke and Asparagus Salad *(page 180)*

Potatoes Cooked in the Coals *(page 81)*

Rhubarb Cobbler *(page 228)*

resources

American Community Gardening Association (page 54)
1777 East Broad St.
Columbus, OH 43203
877-ASK-ACGA or 877-275-2242
www.communitygarden.org
Find a community garden locally

Eat Local Challenge
www.eatlocalchallenge.com
A group blog written by authors who are interested in the benefits of eating food grown and produced in their local foodshed

Eat Wild (page 179)
9609 SW 288th St.
Vashon, WA 98070
866-453-8489
www.eatwild.com
Provides information about and links consumers to local suppliers of grass-fed meat

Ecological Farming Association
406 Main St., Suite 313
Watsonville, CA 95076
831-763-2111
www.eco-farm.org
Dedicated to the development of ecologically based food systems, both domestically and throughout the world

Edible Communities
369 Montezuma Ave., Suite 577
Santa Fe, NM 87501
505-989-8822
www.ediblecommunities.com
Excellent community-based local food publications

Farm Aid
11 Ward St., Suite 200
Somerville, MA 02143
617-354-2922
www.farmaid.org
Promotes food from family farms through their annual farm-benefit concert and other multimedia campaigns

Farm to School
www.farmtoschool.org
Programs across the USA that connect schools with local farms

Food Routes
P.O. Box 55-35 Apple Lane
Arnot, PA 16911
570-638-3608
www.foodroutes.org
Information about buying fresh, local, and organic food

Local Harvest (pages 15 and 55)
220 21st Ave.
Santa Cruz, CA 95062
831-475-8150
www.localharvest.org
Information on local family farms, farmers' markets, CSAs, and other sources of sustainably grown food and grass-fed meats in your area

Monterey Bay Aquarium and Seafood Watch (page 129)
886 Cannery Row
Monterey, CA 93940
831-648-4888
www.seafoodwatch.org
This world-renowned aquarium runs the Seafood Watch program to help consumers find seafood from sustainable sources

Outstanding in the Field
P.O. Box 2413
Santa Cruz, CA 95062
www.outstandinginthefield.com
For information about upcoming dinners and a look back at past dinners and the chefs, winemakers, producers, and artisans who have participated in them

Slow Food
www.slowfood.com
International nonprofit organization focused on protecting food traditions and culture

United States Department of Agriculture Agricultural Marketing Service
www.ams.usda.gov/farmersmarkets/map.htm
An interactive website and map with lists of farmers' markets by state, city, and county

United States Government Environmental Protection Agency
www.epa.gov/pesticides/food
For information concerning pesticides and food, health and safety issues

Wild Farm Alliance
P.O. Box 2570
Watsonville, CA 95077
831-761-8408
www.wildfarmalliance.org
Promotes farming that protects wildlife habitat, reconnecting food systems with ecosystems

Wine Resources (page 145)
Appellation America:
   www.appellationamerica.com
All American Wineries:
   www.allamericanwineries.com
Weekend Winery: www.weekendwinery.com
   State-by-state listings of local wine producers

charitable organizations

MANY of our dinners have been benefits for local organizations that support organic farming, agricultural sustainability, or school or community causes. These worthy organizations include:

Berkshire Grown (page 224)
P.O. Box 983
Great Barrington, MA 01230
413-528-0041
www.berkshiregrown.org
Supports local food and farms in the Berkshire region of Massachusetts, New York, Vermont, and Connecticut

Colorado Organic Producers Association (COPA)
2727 CR 134
Hesperus, CO 81326
970-588-2292
www.organiccolorado.org
Provides information and networking services to promote Colorado organic food products

Community Alliance with Family Farmers (CAFF)
36355 Russell Blvd.
Davis, CA 95616
www.caff.org
Supports family-scale, sustainable, organic agriculture, and CSAs to build stronger communities

Chez Panisse Foundation (page 20)
1517 Shattuck Ave.
Berkeley, CA 94709
510-843-3811
www.chezpanissefoundation.org
Funds a great variety of education initiatives, including the Edible Schoolyard

First Slice
4401 N. Ravenswood
Chicago, IL 60640
773-506-1719
www.firstslice.org
Provides meals prepared using local, organic ingredients to low-income families in Chicago

Friends of the University of California Santa Cruz Farm & Garden at the Center for Agroecology & Sustainable Food Systems
1156 High St.
Santa Cruz, CA 95064
831-459-3240
casfs.ucsc.edu/community/friends.html
Supports the work of the University Agroecology program

Green City Market
820 Davis St., Suite 134
Evanston, IL 60201
847-424-2486
www.chicagogreencitymarket.org
This Chicago market connects local producers and farmers to chefs, restaurateurs, food organizations, and the public

Just Food (page 54)
208 East 51st St., 4th Fl.
New York, NY 10022
212-645-9880
www.justfood.org
Supports the development of a sustainable food system, encompassing New York City–area family farms, community gardeners, and communities

La Plaza Cultural Community Garden (page 54)
East Ninth St. and Avenue C
New York, NY 10009
www.laplazacultural.org
A garden oasis in the big city, La Plaza Cultural hosts plays, picnics, volunteer work parties, and community children's programs

Marin Organic
P.O. Box 962
Pt. Reyes Station, CA 94956
415-663-9667
www.marinorganic.org
A cooperative association of Marin County organic producers dedicated to creating and preserving a sustainable local food system

Northeast Organic Farming Association (NOFA)
Box 135
Stevenson, CT 06491
203-888-5146
www.nofa.org
Promotes healthy food and organic farming in the northeast region of the United States

Open Space Alliance of Santa Cruz
P.O. Box 8042
Santa Cruz, CA 95061
831-423-0700
www.santacruzosa.org
Protects farmlands and wildlife habitat in Santa Cruz County, California

Parkway Partners
1137 Baronne St.
New Orleans, LA 70113
504-620-2224
www.parkwaypartnersnola.org
Improves green space and promotes community gardens in New Orleans

Peconic Land Trust
296 Hampton Rd.
P.O. Box 1776
Southampton, NY 11969
631-283-3195
www.peconiclandtrust.org
Works to protect Long Island's farms, natural lands, and heritage

Slow Food L.A.
http://www.slowfoodla.com
Promotes slow-food events and activities in the Los Angeles area

Southern Sustainable Agriculture Working Group
http://www.ssawg.org
Advocates for sustainable agriculture in the South

Stone Barns Center for Food and Agriculture (page 13)
630 Bedford Rd.
Pocantico Hills, NY 10591
914-366-6200
www.stonebarnscenter.org
Nonprofit farm, educational center, and restaurant demonstrate and promote sustainable, community-based food production

Sustainable Nantucket
P.O. Box 1244
Nantucket, MA 02554
508-228-3399
www.sustainablenantucket.org
Works to preserve the culture, heritage, agriculture, and fishery and harbors of Nantucket Island

UBC Farm at the University of British Columbia (page 39)
The University of British Columbia
2357 Main Mall
Vancouver, BC V6T 1Z4
604-822-5092
www.landfood.ubc.ca/ubcfarm
A teaching, research, and community farm located on the urban university campus in Vancouver

Wattles Farm
1714 Curson Ave.
Hollywood, CA 90046
One of the oldest community gardens in Los Angeles

acknowledgments

SINCE our original dinner in the field in 1999, literally thousands of people have contributed to the traveling adventure that is called Outstanding in the Field. From the beginning our goal has been to recognize and acknowledge producers and artisans whose skill and hard work bring good food to the table. Thanking those who have helped in the genesis and completion of this book must begin with the farmers, the fishermen, the cheesemakers, the ranchers, the foragers and beekeepers, and the winemakers. It is these folks who have brought substance and meaning to the work of Outstanding in the Field.

Andy Griffin and Julia Wiley of Mariquita Farm were first; their kindness and generosity gave us confidence to continue. Farmer Bill Denevan, oldest of my seven brothers, brought us our second site, set among the just-ripe apples of his Happy Valley Orchard; he regaled us with fascinating stories of the orchard around the Thanksgiving and Christmas table. Thanks to Greg Beccio of Happy Boy Farm who invited us to the last and most remote of our dinner sites of our first season.

I am deeply grateful to the following farmers across North America who over many fruitful seasons have generously welcomed us into their fields: Jack Algiere, Stone Barns Center for Food and Agriculture; John Bartlett, Bartlett's Ocean View Farm; Mark Bomford and Gavin Wright, UBC Farm; Thomas and Constance Broz, Live Earth Farm; Larry Butler and Carol Ann Sayle, Boggy Creek Farm; Scott Chasky, Quail Hill Community Farm; Tom and Nancy Clark, Old Chatham Sheep Herding Farm; David Cleverdon, Kinnikinnick Farm; Jim Cochran, Swanton Berry Farm; Bill and Romeo Coleman, Coleman Farm; Al Courchesne, Frog Hollow Farm; David Evans, Marin Sun Farms; Rich and Laura Everett, Everett Family Farm; Lou Johns, Blue Heron Farm; Rick and Kristi Knoll, Knoll Farm; Don Lareau and Daphne Yannakakis, Zephyros Farm; Jeff Larkey, Route One Farm; Barry Logan, La Milpa Organica Farm; Jason Mann, Full Moon Farms; Eberhard Müller and Paulette Satur, Satur Farm; Mark Pasternak, Devil's Gulch Ranch; Steve Pederson, High Ground Organics; David Retsky, County Line Harvest; Brandon Ross, Ella Bella Farm; Joe Schirmer, Dirty Girl Farm; Vern Stockwell, Stockwell Farm; Tucker Taylor, Woodland Gardens; Jerry and Jean Thomas, Thomas Farm; Deborah Walton, Canvas Ranch; and Warren Webber, Star Route Farm.

Vintners have also hosted several dinners, including Alexis Bailly, Alexis Bailly Vineyard; Randall Grahm, Bonny Doon Vineyard; Robert Haas, Tablas Creek Vineyard; Chuck Smith and Mary Berry-Smith, Smith-Berry Vineyard; John Williams, Frog's Leap Vineyard.

Our beautiful garden dinner sites include La Plaza Cultural de Armando Perez in New York City; Parkway Partners Community Garden in New Orleans; Strawberry Banke in Portsmouth, New Hampshire; and Wattles Farm in Hollywood, California.

I am humbly grateful to our participating farm dinner guest chefs, our regional ambassadors who share a deep appreciation for and interest in fostering a culinary sense of place. Chefs include Tamar Adler, Alejandro Alcocer, Michael Anthony, Nate Appleman, Sean Baker, Dan Barber, Jennifer Biesty, Kathy Cary, Seth Caswell, Terry Conlan, Robert Cubberly, Brian Curry, Traci Des Jardins, Mary Dumont, Duskie Estes, Corbin Evans, Tom Fundaro, Gabrielle Hamilton, David Hawksworth, Malika Henderson, Mick Hug, Paul Kahan, David Kinch, Evan Kleiman, Remi Lauvand, Daniel Long, Joseph Manzare, Tom McNary, Richard Mead, Justine Miner, Kris Morningstar, Jonah Oakden, Cory Obenour, Sean O'Brien, Melissa Perello, Charles Phan, Anne Quatrano, Marc Rasic, Seth and Angela Raynor, Louis Rossman, Lenny Russo, Jason Seibert, Justin Severino, Jamie Smith, Susan Spicer, Craig Stoll,

Johnathan Sundstrom, Damani Thomas, Nicci Tripp, Eric Tucker, Michael Tusk, Paul Virant, J. Bryce Whittlesey, and Randy Windham. Thank you for sharing our vision.

Thanks to Alice Waters for joining us for dinner in the peach orchard. Her work has inspired us to go to new and interesting places.

Paul Cocking, owner of Gabriella Café in Santa Cruz, provided invaluable help and support with the restaurant's first farm dinners, which grew into Outstanding in the Field.

Outstanding in the Field began in 1999 with three core people: Chef Tom King, Manager Julia Belanger, and myself. We all were eager to introduce a new idea (yet as I have mentioned before, an idea that is also quite old) of dining at the source of the meal. Tom had the reckless whimsy to partner with me and take on such a challenging culinary project. Julia had the difficult task of attempting to have it all make financial sense.

Soon Web Geisha and budding photographer Tana Butler arrived and, taken by these strange quixotic chefs, worked tirelessly to carve out a website that would spread the news.

Our family quickly grew. In season two, Katharine Stern joined us in the field as co-chef. Season three saw Leah Talbott became our field manager as we found ever greater interest in our mission. Leah guided us through a very busy season as we expanded to varied farm locations throughout the Bay Area.

With season four came Jane Freedman, an experienced respected organic farmer, who lent her considerable organizational expertise to our new ambition to go even further afield; that year we put together our first East Coast Outstanding in the Field event, at the Stone Barns Center for Food and Agriculture.

Season five began the Outstanding in the Field that exists today. Katy Oursler took over as field manager, and soon we had a full cross-country schedule and a bright red and white bus. Katy stuck it out through thick and thin, including our bus breakdown in the wilds of the Yukon Territory of Canada. Thank you, Katy, for your warm and welcoming presence at the dinners and especially for your all-around hard work. We couldn't and wouldn't have done it without you.

I am very grateful to the Outstanding staff that has joined Katy and me on the bus for our North American tour during one or more of the past several seasons: Barry Boullion, Caleb Coe, Noelle Darling, Wyatt Dexter, Natalie Mock, Leah Scafe, Katherine Schimmel, and Veronica Schultz. Your getting on the bus has made a big difference.

Chef Katherine Stern has provided invaluable and continuing culinary inspiration. Many of the recipes in the book evolved both out of our years of working together at Gabriella Café and from working as co-chefs during our second season.

Many thanks to Marah Stets, my patient and talented cowriter, who bravely ventured into a dense and far-ranging thicket of farm and food stories. I hope you can join us on the bus when we venture further afield with new journeys to ever more exotic and mysterious continents.

Thanks to photographers Andrea Wyner, Alexandra Grablewski, and Wyatt Dexter. With your help, all can see how beautiful and meaningful this project has become.

To my skilled editor at Clarkson Potter, Rica Allannic, thanks for having great faith in the project even when it sometimes involved tracking me down (at the beach or on the road) to keep things moving.

Thanks finally to my young son, Brighton. Many thanks for contributing eggs from your small flock of chickens for our dinner at Route One . . . and the wild mushrooms, too. Our trip to the far reaches of Alaska for a farm dinner is a father-son journey I will always remember.

index